D1541764

The
PICTURE
FRAMER'S
Handbook

The
PICTURE
FRAMER'S
Handbook

Michael Woods

B.T. Batsford Ltd, London

To the memory of my Father, Reginald Woods, MBE, who first encouraged my use of his workshop

ISBN 0 7134 5779 1 (cased)
ISBN 0 7134 5780 5 (limp)

Typeset by Servis Filmsetting Limited
and printed in Great Britain by
Courier International Ltd Tiptree Essex

for the publishers B. T. Batsford Ltd
4 Fitzhardinge Street
London W1H OAH

Acknowledgements

I would like to thank Mary Macdonald for allowing me to photograph her two lace pictures (figs 78 and 79); Wendy Pringle for her samples of traditional lace (fig. 75); Rosina Barnard for her embroidery (figs 15 and 81); Charlotte Stagg for allowing me to borrow her pressed flowers (fig. 71); Shoot of Godalming for developing and printing my films; and, of course, my wife for checking and typing the manuscript.

Contents

Introduction

It is a magic moment when you hang a picture on a wall. Suddenly the wall becomes relatively unimportant and it seems as if a new window has been let into it. The picture might be a reminder of a most happy holiday – a painting full of colour or a treasured find from a market stall. No matter what it is, it will be special and important to you.

Yet, all too frequently, those feelings, and the enjoyment of looking and looking over the months ahead are limited to only one or two places in a house. This is not because pictures are disliked, but the task, and sometimes the unknown cost, of framing is offputting. But it is very simple to mount and frame pictures.

Probably one particular possession will start you off, but when that has been framed and is proudly on a wall, the fever starts. What else can be framed? There are so many possibilities (fig. 2): magazines (which sometimes produce special pages with framing in mind, embroidered samplers, posters, children's drawings, stamps, illustrations from old and broken books, old postcards, your own paintings, etc. There are also possibilities beyond the two dimensional; medals and buttons, shells and dried or pressed flowers, patterned tiles and old tools can all be considered.

I refer to hanging pictures in Chapter 7, but when thinking about what you want to do and what to choose, I should certainly make a plea for a wall somewhere in the house which will take eight or twelve small, but all differently framed, pictures or objects (fig. 3). There one by one you can hang your frames, compare styles and consider your own likes and dislikes. Many shops sell ready-made frames in a great variety of styles, while the local sale-room or other second-hand source will yield a promising supply. However, the choice of style, treatment and the final presentation of the framed work is, in the end, yours.

3 A collection of pictures, framed in various
ways. The surrounding space allows for more
frames to be added later

TYPES OF FRAMING

Chapter 1
TYPES OF FRAMING

There are no absolute rules when it comes to framing; a good frame is one which complements your picture. However, a few guidelines may be helpful.

Oil paintings on canvas

A simple batten – that is, a strip of wood or metal attached to the outer edge of the stretcher – will not cover any of the picture (fig. 4). A frame with a rabbet should cover cover only as much of the picture as is needed to hold it in place (fig. 5). A frame with a moulding needs to be of a generous width, for if it is too thin it will appear rather petty; it is better to have a single thin edge if you cannot use a generous moulding. The apparent size of a frame can be increased by using a slip – usually a flat strip of wood added to the frame's section on the picture side (fig. 6). Though much smaller, a slip on an oil painting might be compared with the mount on a watercolour.

5 *The backs of two old frames. The right-hand frame has a rabbet which would cover far too much of a painting. The left-hand frame has better proportions and the stretcher could still be expanded to tighten the canvas*

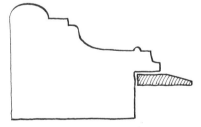

6 *Larger sectioned frames are often composed of more than one element – the innermost one is called a slip*

4 *An oil painting on canvas with a simple wood batten*

Watercolours

Traditionally, watercolours have thin frames and wide mounts. If the edge of the watercolour is not covered by the mount, the work will look lighter, freer, possibly more vigorous, but not so realistic; the random edge will show the paint quality (fig. 7). If the mount covers the edge, the work will look tighter, less vigorous, but more realistic; the effect of 'the window' onto the view will be increased (fig. 8).

Drawings

The question of whether the edge of the drawing should be seen (fig. 9) or just covered (fig. 10) requires the same consideration as for a watercolour. When in doubt, it is probably best to let the drawing breathe and allow the whole of it to be seen.

Prints – etchings, silk screen prints, lithographs

Though you may choose otherwise, it is traditional to show the edge of the print (fig. 11); in fact, the edge shows the skill of the printmaker and should be crisp. An etching should show the edge of the plate as well; this appears as a round-corenered rectangular dent, made when the damp paper was pressed onto the plate (fig. 12). The lithograph in (fig. 13) has a printing registration mark which needs to be covered.

Prints of the mass-produced type can be treated in any manner. Sometimes these have oddly proportioned white edges (postcards, for example) while others may have printed information at the bottom. If you have to have bare paper at the bottom, then leave a comfortable amount on the other sides as well; if not, give the picture total importance and mount or frame it precisely at the picture's edge.

Photographs

These look best when trimmed (showing no white border round the edge) and mounted onto card using a rubber-based glue or photographers' spray mounting preparation. Generally it is best to show the whole composition, letting the edge of the photograph be seen (fig. 14).

Three-dimensional objects

The frame is virtually a setting for the object or group of objects which will be fixed to a plain centre panel. The frame will have to have sufficient depth to accommodate the objects if glass or plastic is used for protection. Tapestry, lace and pressed flowers will, according to their thickness, require various treatments; for example, a tapestry could be treated as an oil painting on canvas (fig. 15). However, the mounting and framing should be secondary and not be allowed to overwhelm the strong textures shown.

7 A watercolour with trial pieces of mounting card allowing the edge marks to show

8 The same watercolour as in fig. 7, but with the edge marks covered

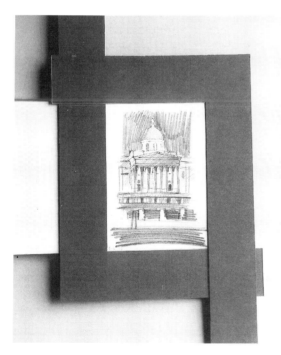

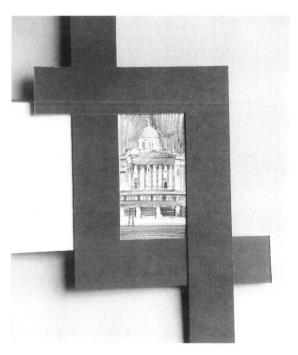

9 A drawing with its shaded edges exposed

10 The same drawing as in fig. 9, but with the trial mount covering the loose edge to create a tight rectangle

12 *An etching with its printed edge showing. The reverse side of the print shows the mark of the plate in the paper. This mark is traditionally seen even if the picture does not occupy the whole plate*

13 *The edge of a lithograph should be seen but the registration marks, used for alignment during the printing process, should be covered*

14 A photograph looks best trimmed of its white edges and mounted. This example is mounted on a 15 mm ($\frac{1}{2}$ in.) block which gives it a chunky quality

15 A sample of embroidery which is not flat.
When presented, it should be lightly tensioned.
(See Chapter 5)

TYPES OF FRAMING

Chapter 2

THE WORK AREA

Where to work

Frame-making can be undertaken by anybody who might not normally have a work room. It is not a dirty occupation – sawdust is very easily swept up – and most frames will lie on an opened-out newspaper. Initially, the uncut lengths of wood may be very long, so a large room or a small one with a well-placed door or window will enable the first cuts to be made. A sturdy table which you can clamp a vice to is very important. Small, mobile work benches might serve, though there is a degree of calmness gained by being able to spread out all the materials on a good, large, rectangular table, about 1.5 × 1.2 m (5 × 4 ft).

Work surfaces and lighting

Choose as flat a surface as possible, with no open joints; any superficial cracks and waves can complicate simple jobs. If you do have to cover a table with a 'work surface' use a sheet of compressed chipboard with some old material stuck on the back to prevent scratching; devise an edge to overlap and put the temporary top on the table to prevent it moving.

A shelf in easy reach nearby, or another small table at about the same height as the main table, is also invaluable (a mobile kitchen trolley would be ideal); you can keep tools on it close at hand without interfering with the actual work. Lighting from an adjustable spotlight is also an asset (figs 16 and 17).

It is very useful to be able to leave your frame just where it is – to dry or to await a next stage. Where possible, give this aspect priority. As you become involved with mounting and framing you will find that a mini-production line can be an advantage. Being able to repeat one process several times will be enormously valuable, and your standards and judgements will improve more quickly.

16 *A work area with an adjustable lamp and a tool trolley*

THE WORK AREA

17a A bradawl – it can be given a more useful, thinner point by filing it

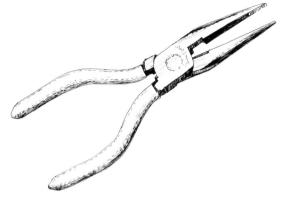

17b Pliers – pointed ends and a wire-cutting slot are an advantage

17c A large-handled craft knife, with replaceable blades

17d A tenon saw with particularly fine teeth; coarse teeth can chip the mitre edges

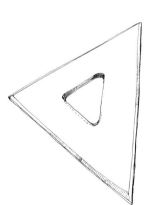

17e A transparent set square – an aid to making rectangles

Chapter 3

MOUNTS

A mount is a surround to a drawing which gives it space to breathe; it provides an area of calm so that you can focus on the work itself (fig. 18). Normally, mounts are made of special card – stiff and thick, yet easy to cut. However you do not necessarily have to use this special material to considerably improve a drawing. Many people produce work in quantity, and to frame just one piece for all time is hardly sensible, so to begin with try the following treatment.

Backing paper mounts

Using a ruler and set-square, draw a rectangle on the drawing sheet which will enable the drawing-pin holes and bent-over corners to be removed. With a metal straight-edge or metal ruler (a 1 m (3 ft) length is essential for anything but the smallest of pictures) and a craft knife, cut off the unwanted edges. Clean up any easily-removed unwanted marks, possibly re-

sign and date the work closer in to the drawing if it is yours, or get the artist to do so if it isn't.

Select a frame at least 100 mm (4 in.) larger than your trimmed drawing sheet (see Chapter 4 for types of frames). Cut your backing sheet to suit the frame, choosing any white or coloured paper you particularly like. With two tiny pieces of self-adhesive putty, one at each top corner, place the drawing down onto the backing paper. Check that the picture is centrally placed (if any extra space is available make the bottom border the largest).

With a 2B or 3B pencil and ruler, mark out and draw a single pencil line on the backing paper, about 10 mm ($\frac{3}{8}$ in.) from the drawing edge. I keep a stick of 10 mm ($\frac{3}{8}$ in.) square wood for just this purpose of drawing a surrounding line. With one side resting against the actual paper edge, the pencil line can be drawn on the other side of the stick (fig. 19). This method is very simple and surprisingly effective; and, if

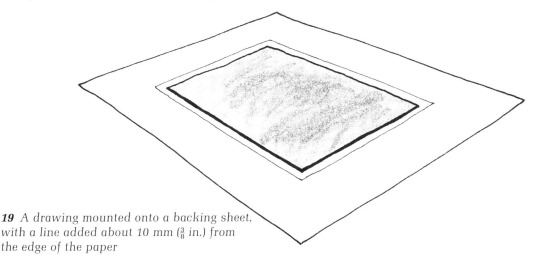

19 *A drawing mounted onto a backing sheet, with a line added about 10 mm ($\frac{3}{8}$ in.) from the edge of the paper*

using the same frame you wish to change the drawing and have a different border, it will take only 15 minutes. This paper border is ideal when used in conjunction with the 'no-frame' method described in Chapter 5. If a traditional section frame is used, you can fix turning clips at the back, making access much quicker.

Card mounts

A cut-card mount involves the same questions of size, proportion and colour as a backing paper mount but gives a more permanent and considerably richer feeling because of the thickness of the mounting card which is revealed when it is cut with a bevelled edge.

Mounting card is produced in a very wide range of colours. In order to decide which shade to choose, test the colours against the picture. Make a collection of samples: pieces of old mounting card, card painted with different emulsion paints, pieces of wrapping paper, cuttings from cardboard boxes – the wider the range of samples the better.

If you arrange four strips around the picture (four 100 mm (4 in.) strips 600 mm (2 ft) long will be a useful guide) you can get a rough impression of the colour. Although light off-white colours can be bright and fresh, they do not show off some pale watercolours well, and it is worth trying dark tones – a holly green, a dark sepia brown or a gunmetal grey – which can look very rich. The frame and wall against which it is to be seen must also be taken into account, for though the picture is, of course, very important, it is the relationship of colour, tone, size and lighting which determines

whether the framing looks tired or alive.

Consider the item to be mounted very carefully, taking into account the points made in Chapter 1. Two L-shaped pieces of mounting card (fig. 20) are very useful to determine the exact picture area wanted, which will be the same as the rectangle to be cut in the mount. Write this size down. To each of the two dimensions add 150 mm (6 in.), i.e. a picture size seen 250 $\times$ 500 mm (10 $\times$ 20 in.) will require a piece of mounting card 250 + 150 $\times$ 500 + 150 = 400 $\times$ 650 mm (10 + 6 $\times$ 20 + 6 = 16 $\times$ 26 in.).

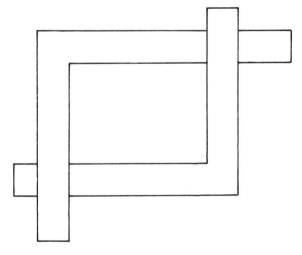

20 *Two L-shaped pieces of mounting card used for determining the picture area. (These could be made from an unwanted mount cut at two opposite corners)*

Cutting
Consider the most economical placing of the size needed on your whole sheet of mounting

card and mark it out on the side you will see (the coloured side). Place the card colour-side up, on your smooth, clean, flat table; with your knife, cut off the piece you have marked. Long thin off-cuts are useful as a surface on which to cut. Refresh your memory as to the dimensions of the opening you require and, well away from the corners of the mount you are to cut, mark the sides 75 mm (3 in.) from the left and right on the seen face. Next turn the card round through 90° so that the left-hand side, which might be described as nine o'clock, is brought to a six o'clock position. Line up your ruler's left hand end with the mount's future top and with the two dots recently made. Draw the line 70 mm ($2\frac{3}{4}$ in.) from the left and terminate it 85 mm ($3\frac{1}{4}$ in.) before reaching the right – which, of course, will actually be the base of the mount. Move the ruler upwards and repeat the making of the side lines exactly (fig. 21). Then return the mounting card to its correct position and simply connect the top and bottom ends of the two side lines.

Because the marking has to be done on the actual face of the mounting card, take care not to put the dots or lines where they are not wanted; a pencil will actually dent mounting card and rubbing out will not remove the dent, only mar the surface!

With nothing in the way behind you, and with a brand new blade in your craft knife, hold the knife leaning over to the right (if you are right-handed), with the blade at approximately 45° to the surface of the card (figs 22 and 23). The tip of the blade should lie just to the right, or outside edge, of the line so that you can see it as you cut. Adjust your light. The marked

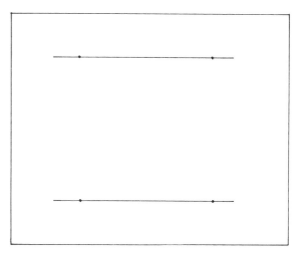

21 A mount with a vertical format. Two dots left and two dots right are used to draw lines for the left and right sides; the length of these sides will be the top and bottom edges of the mount

line itself will be left on the centre piece which is being removed. Lean forward but be prepared to move your body backwards, without moving your feet. Make an incision right through the thickness of the card – you want to cut only once – and then, keeping your arm tense, draw the whole of your body backwards and cut down the length of the line to the corner. Take the knife out. Turn the card through 90° anti-clockwise so that you prepare to continue the cut down the next side, following on from the first. Make the incision and, drawing your body and arm back together, make the second cut – all the time keeping your eye on the pencil line. In a similar fashion cut the third and fourth sides, finally returning to the corner at which you started.

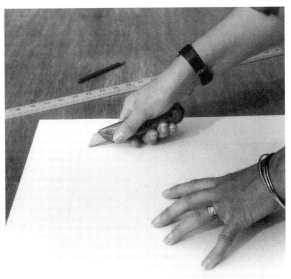

22 Hold the craft knife, with a new blade, at an angle to the card surface. Do not use a dirty blade – for example, sharpening a pencil can leave a dirty residue

23 The actual hand-hold can vary, but it must be firm. Your knuckles should run along the card surface and your thumb can also touch the card. Ensure your hands are clean and dry!

It is unlikely that the centre piece will immediately drop out, for almost certainly little pices of card will remain uncut just at the corners. So, taking great care to re-enter the cut at exactly the same angle with the knife, hold the mounting card in the air and re-cut the card both ways into the corner (fig. 24); you will suddenly feel the mount free. Repeat with the other three corners and remove the centre. The card edge will be very sharp (sharp enough to cut your finger, so take care). Any slight whiskers of paper are best pressed down, or back and under, rather than cut off – you will only damage the crisp edge if you do try to cut them. If you are not satisfied with some wobbly

cuts, and you are able to fix a long metal straight-edge or ruler to your table under which the card can be slipped, you will find that this will give considerably more support to the angled cutting blade and, therefore, guidance for a straight line. However, this will not necessarily produce perfect results – I often feel that rulers can produce beautifully straight lines in the wrong place! Using a ruler or straight-edge without it being screwed down is nearly impossible, for it is very difficult to hold both the mounting card and the ruler while trying to cut at an angle simultaneously.

There are a number of proprietary brands of

mount cutters available which range from hand-held units to the more complex systems used in light industry. I find, however, that these special tools are all a little too sophisticated for the needs of most amateur framers. There is a special pleasure about being able to control one's own hand with a straightforward cutting blade and, if not perfect, the results are usually quite acceptable and will improve noticeably with practice.

Card quality does vary. For a beginner this need hardly be of concern, but when long-term durability is important, acid-free paper and card should be used, which will not become spot-marked with age.

24 Re-enter the cut to free the corner of the rectangle

So, with your picture lying flat on the table, try the mount on it.

Attaching the drawing to the mount

There are various methods of fixing the drawing to the mount (fig. 25).

25a A drawing directly fixed to the back of the mount

25b A drawing fixed to the backing card with a separate mount

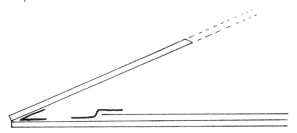

25c A drawing fixed to the backing card with a hinged mount

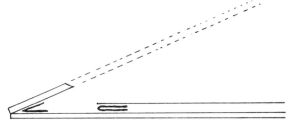

25d A drawing hinged to the backing card (or all corners could be fixed) so that the mount remains clear of the drawing paper

Method A

Place the drawing face down on a clean surface. Along the top edge stick a length of water-based glued paper by wetting half its width (fig. 26). (Do not use transparent adhesive tape for it sticks too immediately, stains, and, in time, becomes brittle.) Turn the drawing over and make a trial positioning of the mount; then, when you have found the ideal place, wet the remaining portion of the glued paper and lay the mount onto the drawing (fig. 27), giving it a gentle pressure with your fist to aid firm adhesion between the wetted glued paper and the back of the mount. Pick up the mount (the drawing should come with it, but will tend to hinge down). Turn the whole mount over and re-press the sticky paper to the back of the mounting card. The drawing fixed in this way will expand and contract with temperature variations. Fixing all round could well produce wrinkles across its surface.

Method B

Fix the work to the backing card with glued paper placed alongside the topmost edge of the drawing. The mount can remain a separate part or be hinged as in Method C. This might be suitable, for instance, where written notes appear on the side of a drawing and, while not wanted for display, could be more easily revealed if the covering mount was not fixed to the drawing (fig. 25b).

Method C

Measure the part of the drawing to be displayed and then prepare the mount. Hinge the mount to the backing card with tape or gummed paper. When the drawing is placed

under the mount, you can adjust its position and, when satisfactory, carefully lift the mount in order to fix the drawing at its top with gummed paper. The mount can then drop back (fig. 28).

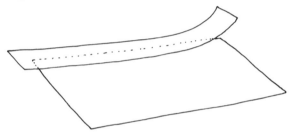

26 *Water-based glued paper. Minimum contact with the drawing paper is desirable*

27 *A mount being lowered onto the drawing*

28 *A hinged mount with the drawing fixed to the backing card*

Method D
This method is used for mounting a work where nothing is to be removed and nothing, or only the very minimum, covered. First, measure the drawing or the whole paper size. Decide on the mount size. If the actual paper edge is to be revealed, keep the mount about 5 mm ($\frac{1}{4}$ in.) away from it. Cut a piece of backing card a little larger than the mount; this will allow for slight positioning adjustments. Using the window of the mount, very, very faintly mark the position of the mount on the backing. This will serve as a guide to placing the drawing on the backing. Fold a piece of water-based glued paper down the middle. Stick one side of the fold to the back of the drawing and, wetting the other side, stick the drawing down onto the backing card.

If the whole of the paper's edge is to be seen free of the mount opening, two additional tiny folds of glued paper could be introduced to the two bottom corners. A piece of folded glued paper should then be stuck to the top edge of the mount and, when the second side is wetted, lowered over the drawing on its backing. Any backing which remains in sight beyond the mount can then be trimmed off with a sharp blade (fig. 29).

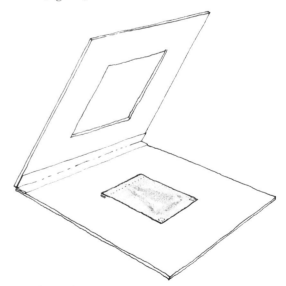

29 *A hinged mount with an opening larger than the work being presented. The work must be lightly fixed at the two bottom points*

Multi-aperture mounts

To show a group of small drawings, it can be quite effective to cut a mount with more than one aperture. Two, three, four, six, nine can be very happily mounted together (fig. 30). As the planning and laying out may be a little more complicated, prepare the whole layout to the exact sizes on a sheet of paper first (fig. 31). It will not matter how many adjustments or wrong marks are made and, when the run through is complete, the paper can be cut to the outside size that you will require your mounting card to be. Cut your mounting card to the same size. Lay the paper on top of the mounting card and keep it in place with metal clips or little pieces of tape taken over to the back. Then, when the paper is fixed, use a pin to prick through the corners of the rectangles to be cut into the card. Remove the paper and, with a fine pencil line, join the points to make the rectangles. Then cut the bevels as before.

30 *A single mount cut with three apertures to present watercolour studies of reflections*

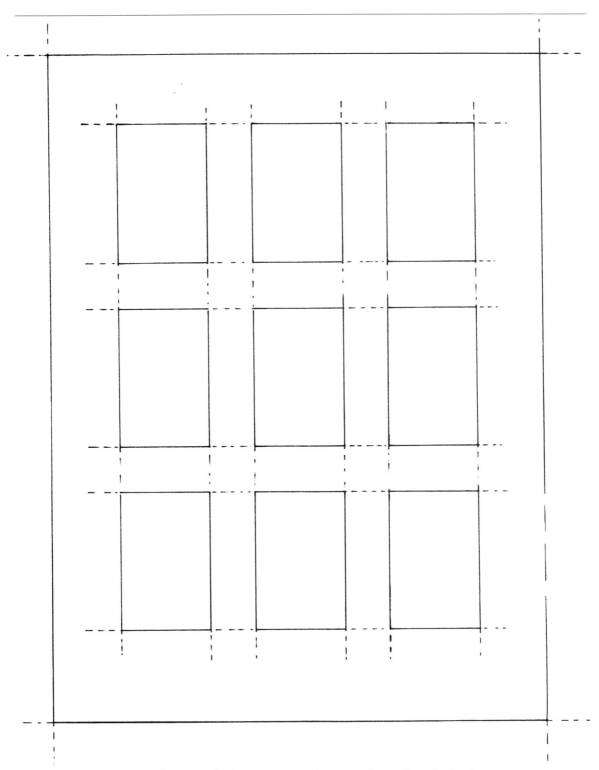

31 A paper preparation sheet on which construction lines can be made. (The final corner positions can be pricked through onto the mounting card)

32 An oval mount is ideal for a portrait

Oval or round mounts

Oval or round mounts can be very attractive if the image is a vignette, i.e., not a firm rectangle but a shape made of the objects drawn (fig. 32); portraits are classic examples.

Once again, I would plan on paper if the marking out is not straightforward. Use a compass for drawing a circle; two compasses, the pointed end of one fixed where the pencil would be in the other, will give you a greater span. Alternatively, use a piece of thin cord tied round a pencil and fixed to a drawing pin, or draw round a bowl or plate which by trial and error may be just the right size.

For an oval, two drawing pins and a loop of thin string will produce many variations of proportions (fig. 33), but, once again, a hunt in the kitchen may suddenly produce convenient ovals, e.g. plates and dishes, gravy boat saucers (fig. 34), even an oval frame itself. In this latter case, to obtain a mount size the same proportion as a frame but smaller in the opening size, use a pencil with a spacing piece of wood taped to it (fig. 35). Carefully run this round the inside of the frame, directly onto the mounting card.

The round or oval mount is cut in the same way as the rectangular sort, except the cut you make must be a curve rather than a straight line, and there are no corners at which to stop in order to turn the card. Therefore, considerable care will be needed when starting to cut again to ensure that the curve of the cut is a smooth one. This will be achieved with a little practice.

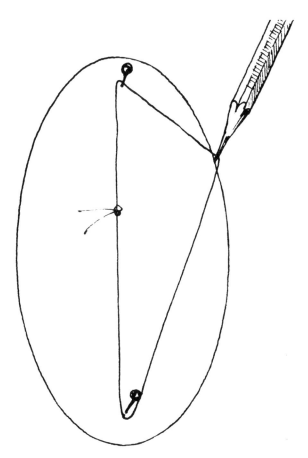

33 Draw an oval by moving a pencil inside a loop of string held in position by two pins. The proportions vary as you alter the gap between the pins and/or the loop size

34 Kitchen utensils provide a supply of instant oval shapes

35 Draw round the inner edge of the oval frame with a pencil taped to a block of wood to create the size of the mount opening

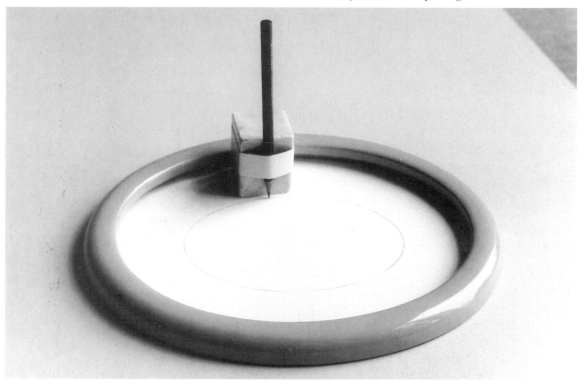

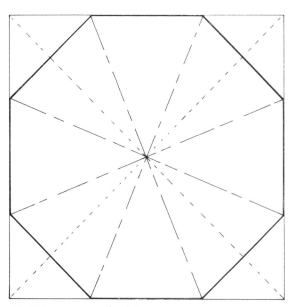

36 *Octagon – method 1*

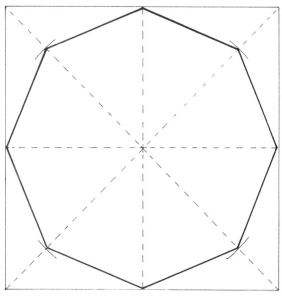

37 *Octagon – method 2*

An easier-to-cut variation of the round mount is an octagon (figs 36 and 37). Construct the octagon in fig. 36 (Method 1) by first drawing a square. Bisect it with diagonals to give it a centre point and then mark off $22\frac{1}{2}°$ divisions from the diagonals. When these are connected, the divisions will be 45°. This construction provides a larger opening than that of Method 2.

Construct the octagon shown in fig. 37 (Method 2) by drawing a square and then dividing it with diagonals, as before. Then divide the square into quarters. With a compass set to a radius just touching the square, mark off the four point onto the diagonals. The octagon can then be completed.

Double Mounts

One method of giving extra richness to a work is to use two mounts. The opening of the second mount is cut, say, 20 mm ($\frac{3}{4}$ in.) bigger than the first, thus mounting the mount. The same colour card or a different colour can be used, but it will be the bevel edge of the mount which will create the lines round the drawing (fig. 38). This is an elaborate version of the pencil line used in the simple mount which is explained earlier in this chapter.

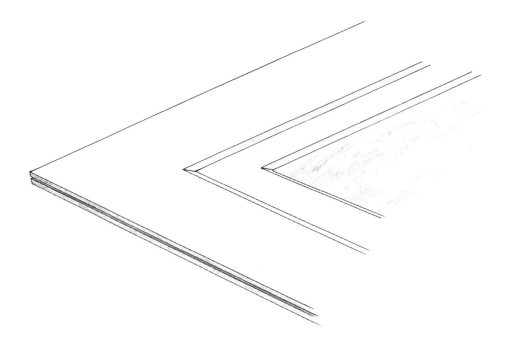

Lined mounts

Pale mounts can be given an extra richness by lines drawn round the opening. Ruling pens holding watercolour are used to create the lines – greys and sepia being more gentle than full black. A draughtsman's stilo-tipped pen is very good for ruling lines – it is easy to use and does not blot. However, a pencil can also be used – although less crisp, it allows for practice with fewer hazards.

A simple marking device is made by cutting a strip of card with a 45° angle. Along the angle make marks at 3 mm ($\frac{1}{8}$ in.) intervals (fig. 39). These can be selected for the spaces required (fig. 40) and repeated very quickly and accurately at each corner with either a pin prick or the tiniest pencil dot.

Laying in a wash

The wash, again of watercolour, is laid between lines with a brush of exactly the same working width (fig. 41). Always experiment on an off-cut of the same mounting card. The density of colour will need to be very thin and it is also essential to prepare more than enough for the area to be laid in, for it will not be possible to re-mix some more half way through without the colour difference and jointings being very obvious. It is also possible to lay in a clear wash of water first to slow the drying process. This can aid a smooth final meeting point where the wash laying begins and ends.

Colours in the picture can be gently echoed in those chosen for the lines and wash. Experiment and practice are needed for these operations, but for certain mounts and pictures the appearance is worth the effort.

Fabric-covered mounts

Covering a card mount with a piece of material can be effective but needs care. The material can create such interest that it overshadows the picture. It is important to consider the decoration of the room when choosing the colour of the mount and frame, but it is a

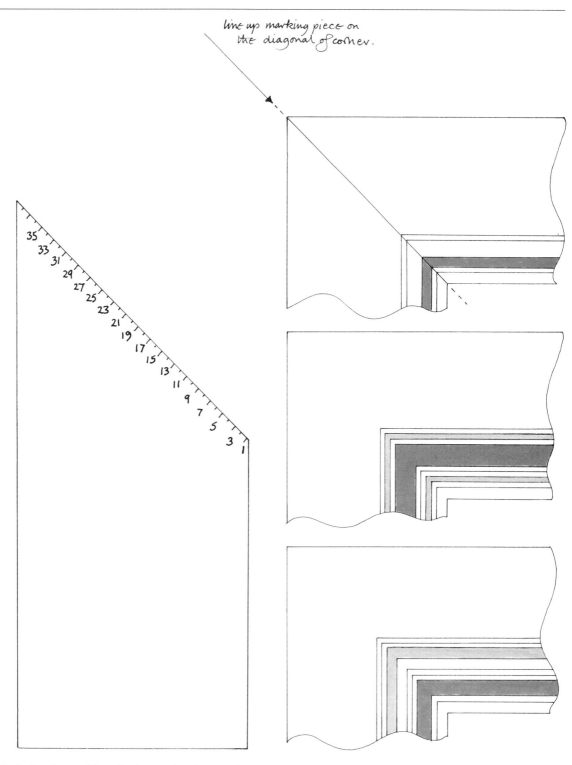

line up marking piece on
the diagonal of corner.

39 A simple marking device made of mounting
card to define the location of wash lines

40 Samples of lines and lines of wash

mistake to think that by making everything match, unity will follow. Material falling in folds in curtains will not look the same when stretched over a chair; so too, material in the flat, rectangular mount, covered by glass, will look different again. Experiment and try alternatives; above all let the drawing or painting remain the most important element.

Cut the mount using the method described earlier. Stretch the material out face down and place the mount on top, taking care to line up any weave with the lines of the mount. Mark round the edges with a soft pencil or tailor's chalk. Remove the mount and draw the cutting lines across what will become the opening. Mark the outside corners of the mount area so that, when brought round to the back of the mount, the fabric will just meet on the corner in a mitre line (i.e. on the diagonal). The angle to the corner will be 45° to the side (fig. 42).

For fixing the material, use a weak, rubber-type glue spread very thinly over the face of the

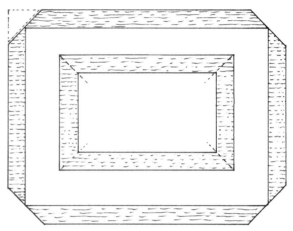

42 Covering a mount (seen from the back)

mount; too much and it will stain the material. Lightly and accurately replace the mount down onto the back of the material, lining it up on the original marks.

Cut out the material with great care at the inside corners; the material must just pull

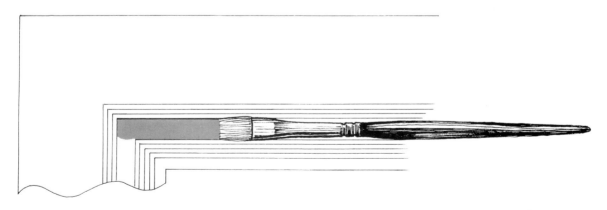

41 Select brushes to suit the desired line width or make the lines to suit your available brushes

43 Mounts covered with decorative wrapping paper. Some types of material, such as plastics and metal foils, may not stick easily, but paper with a dry, matt back is ideal

round the thickness of the mount. Fold the material onto the back and mark it where it will reach. Place glue on those areas, and working on the inside and outside of one side at a time, press the material onto the glue. A length of wood or an old ruler will help to apply pressure evenly over a long length. Do all four sides as quickly as possible. Remove any traces of glue from your fingers and turn the whole mount over. Before the glue dries, tension the material on the back to pull out any wrinkles on the front (fig. 43).

Keep a close eye on the mount while the glue dries. The spring or give in the material will pull the glue until a certain stage of dryness is reached and may cause wrinkling. Double-sided adhesive tape might be suitable for fixing certain types of material.

An oval or circular mount can be covered, but you must cut many little tabs to take the material round the curve to the back (fig. 44). If material with some stretch in its weave can be chosen, this will be found to stick and mould itself to the curve of the card mount more sympathetically. With such a variety of materials available, it would be worth making a small trial first of all.

Finally, if you have occasion to send mounted, but unframed, drawings through the post, or are in any way concerned about their safety in travel, use the centre piece of card from each mount to 're-plug' the hole, thus protecting the work. Only the exact same piece must be used, and replaced exactly the same way round as cut. Acting as a sort of lid, the bevel edge will prevent it pressing through the opening.

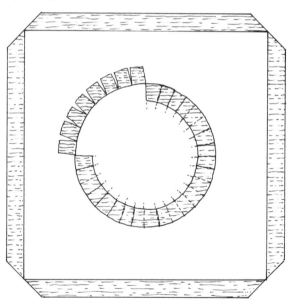

44 A circular mount requires many little tabs to cope with the curve

Chapter 4

MAKING THE FRAME

A painting on a canvas tensioned on a wooden stretcher provides a good starting point for the framer. It allows you to explore the making of mitred corners and see the effect the crisp straight line has on the rather rounded section of the stretcher (fig. 45).

45 *A simple wood batten adds crispness to the rounded form of a canvas*

Battens

A batten is simply a long, thin, flat piece of wood or metal fixed like a thin frame to the edge of a canvas. This is a popular method of framing favoured by students, for when costs have to be kept in check, it both improves the appearance of a painting and gives some protection to rather vulnerable canvas, easily dented when stacked in studios and galleries. The battening, therefore, should stand proud of the face of the canvas by 5–10 mm ($\frac{1}{4}$–$\frac{3}{8}$ in.),

enough to give a projecting, protective edge. Of course, if the painting is going to be hung immediately, then this precautionary element need not be considered, but all the same, the slight projection gives a greater crispness. It also helps to conceal any irregularity at the side of the canvas.

Canvas has to be tucked and folded and tacked in place; with thick canvas this can produce a surprising bulge, and because the battening will touch this, there will inevitably be a slight gap elsewhere. The projection of the battening beyond the face of the canvas will help to minimize the amount this is seen.

Battening 5 mm ($\frac{1}{4}$ in.) wide by 25 mm (1 in.) deep should serve well. Both hard and soft wood can be used. Cutting soft wood is easier; any warpage is less violent, and panel pins are not so likely to split the wood, but knots in soft wood frequently drop right out of such a small, thin section. On the other hand, hard wood will cut crisply, keep its edges and probably be free of large knots, although splits can be more serious.

Buying wood for framing
Buying wood for framing can be alarming. The total length needed for even a little picture is often more than you would imagine. For instance, a 600 mm (24 in.) frame doesn't seem that large until you multiply the length of one side by four. Taking into account the loss when cutting mitres, the final total could be about 2.8 m (9 ft). If you get the sales assistant to cut it into pieces, make certain that each piece is long enough to accommodate the loss on the corner cuts. If you keep the length whole, be careful

how you shop – it is soon possible to get into slapstick situations!

Strange, too, how cars and rooms shrink when wielding lengths of wood and framing! This will be the moment when comments about work area planning come to mean something. For the artist/craftsman a vice (fig. 46) permanently fixed to a table can be a considerable nuisance when involved with other work and certainly this is the case in the improvised work area. It is likely, then, that for a batch of frame-making the vice will be fixed especially. Often, the first chosen position of vice on table and of table in the room will mean that newly-bought wood will not fit the length between wall and mitre box. The trick here is to sight the line of the material being cut to pass through a doorway or window. Later, with shorter pieces, there will be no trouble. If you are cutting battens for the first time, I suggest you begin with a normal straight cut, allowing extra for the mitre to be re-cut later. Naturally, there will be some wood wasted, but it will probably make for a simpler beginning and a successful result. I find these calculations are best done at home, for if a length has not been hastily cut in half in the shop, you might find that five sides are obtainable from one length and a spare piece can save the day when a mistake occurs.

Cutting the mitre

There are a number of clamping and cutting devices available and, though these may help to produce admirable results, I do not think that they are an absolute necessity for a trial start at cutting.

The classic mitre box is a useful tool (fig. 47).

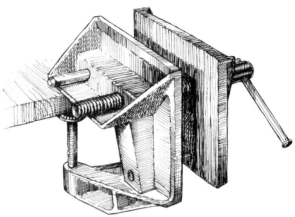

46 This aluminium vice is versatile in its positioning and clamping

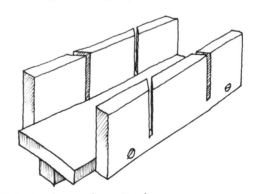

47 A simple wooden mitre box

It should have a block of wood fixed underneath so that it can be gripped in a vice.

With your left hand (reverse each hand position if you are left-handed) hold the wood battening firmly against the far inside of the mitre box; the saw will then travel diagonally across to the right in the guiding slots provided. Always make the cut 5 mm ($\frac{1}{4}$ in.)

from the end of the batten, making certain that a full angle is achieved. If you try to make the cut coincide with the end of the wood you are likely to fail, so waste a little bit and get it right. Make the first cut (fig. 48).

48 *The first mitre being cut*

Place the piece of battening on the table and stand the painting on it. Make an identifying mark on both the batten and the back of the stretcher. Similarly mark the other three sides of the stretcher for later reference. By eye, line up the inside corner of the mitre with the vertical side of the stretcher/painting. Use a straight-edge or ruler placed vertically on the side to help line up the batten; this will reveal the variations of canvas thickness I mentioned earlier, so consider it carefully.

When you are satisfied with that corner, make a pencil mark at the other end where the surplus length will be sticking out; remember that the pencil mark itself will have a width as will the saw cut, but with trial and error, you will get used to this.

Place the battening back in the mitre box with the freshly-cut end sticking out to the left; check that the cut you are about to make will be at the opposite angle to the first. Do not change the direction of the saw in the box; it always is simplest to hold and make your cuts if it travels diagonally to the right. This also means that the outside edge of batten (or frame) will always lie against the far wall of the mitre box. Try the batten against the picture and check both ends.

It is no fault of the frame-maker if the painting is not quite rectangular (unless you are the painter as well). Nevertheless, by the very nature of stretchers and their adjustable corners, it is quite likely that opposite sides will not be the same length. If they are the same length, cut the second side to make a pair exactly the same size as the first and mark it for identification. If they are not the same, the first end should be cut and the second marked against the painting and cut exactly to its dimension. (This will only apply to battening – a proper frame must be made rectangular.) The second paired sides, three and four, should be treated in the same sequence.

Having made all the saw cuts, it is tempting to sandpaper away any whiskers of wood. *Don't!* The corners will be rounded if you do and the crispness spoilt. The whiskers will also help to bed into one another and mask the joint. Any cleaning up should wait until the battening is on the picture. The wood usually used for battening will have such a thin section that joining corners with glue and panel pins will hardly be practical or even necessary. It is at this stage (before assembly) that battening should be painted.

Assembling the batten frame

If no colouring is to be used on the batten, get your hammer and pins within reach of your right hand. Place the painting on the table; standing it on edge, take one appropriate batten (identified by the mark) and lay it along the top edge. Line up the back of the batten with the back of the picture. At the same time, the ends must be aligned; double and triple check this.

When you are happy with the position, using the first finger of your left hand to line up the back of the batten with the back of the stretcher, hammer in one moulding pin about 25 mm (1 in.) from one end, then one similarly positioned at the other end, and at approximately 150 mm (6 in.) intervals along its length. Normally, 20 mm (¾ in.) pins are the best size to use, but it is near the corner that most strength is needed, and longer pins could be used there if necessary.

Place the canvas on a spacing block of wood to raise the jutting mitre from the table surface. Locate the second side (fig. 49). If the canvas in this position is too high for comfortable work, place the spacing block on a lower surface, such as a stool, and replace the canvas, on edge, on the block. With the second side in place, drive in the pins. Continue working your way round, adding the third and fourth sides.

With a piece of fine to medium grade sandpaper wrapped round a flat block of wood, sand the face of the battening at the

corner (fig. 50), and on the outside at the corner. However, never try to round the corner; it will spoil the angle. If the battening is painted, then sandpaper as sparingly as possible; any bared wood can be lightly touched in with the same colour paint.

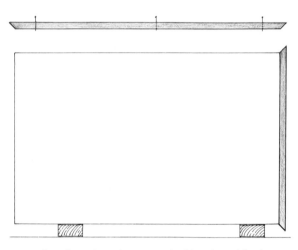

49 *Before locating the second side place blocks under the canvas to prevent damage to the projecting mitre of the first side*

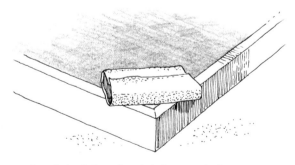

50 *Sand the joint after joining not before*

MAKING THE FRAME

Watercolour frames

Battening is only suitable for oil paintings on canvas; for drawings and watercolours with glass, a frame with a rabbet will be necessary. You may know of local shops which stock a simple wooden frame section. Work out the total length of wood you will need; allow for slightly damaged ends on long lengths and for the extra you will need for cutting the mitres on your frame. Avoid warped lengths.

Cutting the wood

For the beginner, or where space is limited and when there is some length of framing to spare, cut the wood into four basic pieces with a normal right-angled cut. Each piece is going to have two mitred ends. For example, on a frame which has a face of 50 mm (2 in.), allow 60 mm ($2\frac{1}{2}$ in.) for the mitre, times two, in addition to the length of your picture edge. The procedure is the same whether you are framing a canvas or a mounted work, except that canvas (as with battening) produces more lumps and bumps and the exact size is less easy to judge.

When selecting a mounted work, use just the backing card – which must be exactly the same size as the mount – as it will save the actual drawing from possible finger marks. Mark on the back of each piece of wood A and B respectively for the two shorter sides, and C and D for the longer ones (fig. 51). Place A in the mitre box, its back to the far wall of the box, and the frame's face upwards. Cut the right-hand mitre. Remove A from the box and lay the card in the rabbet 2 mm ($\frac{1}{16}$ in.) from the freshly-cut mitre. Mark the other end on the wood and make a little reminder line showing which way

the mitre will travel (fig. 52). (It is very easy to be interrupted and to pick up a marked length of wood with a single dot and proceed to cut it the wrong way!) Place A back in the box, with the back of the frame uppermost. Cut the second mitre. Piece A is now complete. *Do not sandpaper it.*

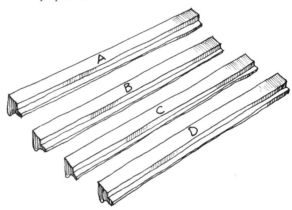

51 *Marking the individual sides saves confusion, but do it on the back of the section*

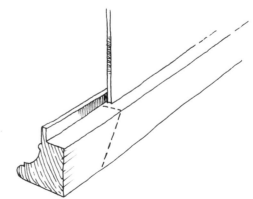

52 *Indicate the direction of the mitre to avoid confusion when cutting the frame*

Select B which will be the opposite piece of the frame. Cut the first mitre as for A, then place A and B outside-edge-to-outside-edge, lining up the two cut mitres to make the shape of a ship's bow. Mark on the back of B the exact point where the mitre of A ends (fig. 53). Place B back in the mitre box, back uppermost, and cut B's second mitre. The second two sides are cut in the same manner.

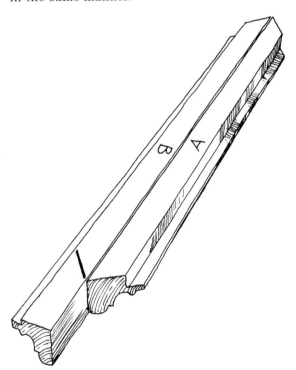

53 Once cut, side A provides the measure for B

When cutting framing with the back upwards, hold it very firmly with your left hand against the far side of the box. All cuts should just leave the mark on the wood of the frame – not the off-cut. It is the side you can see and will be simple enough when you are used to your saw and can judge the width of the cut that it makes.

You should now have four pieces of framing. Two for the shorter sides, A, B, and two for the longer ones, C, D. For an accurate square frame you only have to measure the first side. Very carefully cut sides B, C and D, taking A as the standard. This method of measuring one side against its partner ensures that the finished frame is itself rectangular, even if the mount or canvas may be slightly out of true; the tolerance in the rabbet will take account of any variation. It is worth making a frame for a canvas 3 mm ($\frac{1}{8}$ in.) bigger on each side – the position of the canvas can then be fixed by little pieces of card packed in on each side. Remember, you may need to tighten a canvas by knocking in the stretcher's wedges (see Chapter 7). This will make the whole picture slightly bigger. If you try to cram too large a picture into a frame, a corner may break or the mitre will gape.

Joining the frame

If the picture has a vertical proportion (portrait), select the two shortest pieces, A and B. The corner moulding pins will be driven into these pieces. If the picture has a horizontal proportion (landscape), then select the two longer pieces. The reason for this is that two pins in each corner will be enough for most small frames if some glue is used as well. This makes for a neater appearance from the side, with no pinheads to be seen (one rarely sees the top or bottom of a frame).

Using only enough pressure to hold your frame without damaging its surface or denting it, place it in the vice (wooden face pieces fitted to the vice are valuable here). Drive in two pins so that their points just protrude mid-way along the freshly-cut mitre corner (figs 54 and 55). Their length should be approximately 25–30 mm ($1–1\frac{1}{4}$ in.).

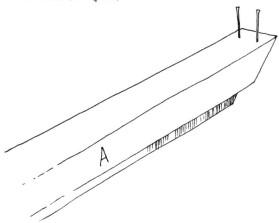

54 *Moulding pins should be located at both ends of A and B before assembling the frame*

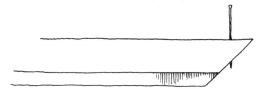

55 *The tip of the pin should just protrude*

Move the frame in the vice to the other end for firm support, and hammer in the other two pins. Similarly, locate the pins in the other side, B. It does rather depend on the section of the frame you are using, but generally you will find that to grip the frame between the outside edge and the edge of the rabbet is the most satisfactory.

Place side D vertically in the vice so that it protrudes about 50 mm (2 in.) above it. Stand to the right of the vice and work to your left. (You will be looking at the back of piece D sticking up in the vice.)

With your hammer to hand, put a small quantity of wood glue onto the mitre surfaces. Then locate piece A onto D, slightly higher on the slope than a perfect match should be (fig. 56) because there is a tendency for piece A to slide downwards as you hit the pin. There is a knack in judging quite how much higher A should be located. If you do not start high enough, by the time you have hammered home the pins, you will find that piece A has slid down past a perfect match and, do what you will, you cannot get it back! The best way is to start 5 mm ($\frac{1}{4}$ in.) high (fig. 57) and still have a fraction to go when the pins are completely in (fig. 58). Then, with a sharp tap of the hammer, move piece A down the last fraction. It is a very nice feeling when you get it just right (fig. 59)! If you think you may dent the edge of the frame doing this, a block of wood interspaced will save damage. Slacken the vice.

Hold both sides of the L piece now assembled and lay it flat on the table. Repeat exactly with piece C in the vice and B being located on top. The two L pieces now have to be brought together with a little more support. If C is held in the vice, with B attached, but without support from below, it will sag. So, with a pile of books (or something similar), just take the weight of the end of B, while the other end of C is about 50 mm (2 in.) above the vice. Put a little glue onto the surface of the mitre and locate the second L shape, A/D (fig. 60); line up the back of the frame, high in position.

Drive home the pins and tap into the exact position for the mitre. With one hand holding the frame at its remaining unjoined corner, slacken off the vice and carefully turn the frame round and replace it in the vice to complete the final corner. Put a little glue into the joint, locate, drive in the pins, give a final tap and the frame is complete.

Clean off any messy glue. Synthetic wood glues can be removed with a water-dampened rag – they look white when applied but colourless when dry. If you can bear to do so, let the frame lie quietly overnight for the glue to dry or cure. If you do try it on your picture be careful not to get glue onto your mount. Leave it until the glue has dried. While this is happening you can measure for and obtain your piece of picture glass, generally 2–3 mm ($\frac{1}{8}$ in.) thick. Allow it to be 3mm ($\frac{1}{8}$ in.) smaller than the rabbet size. For cutting glass yourself, see Chapter 6.

Fitting the picture in the frame

Although until now everything may have gone according to plan, when you come to place the picture in your frame, there may be a moment when, for all the calculations, it does not fit; try turning it round for this may just solve the problem. *If not, don't despair!*

If the mount is slightly too large, with your cutting knife, pare off a sliver on two sides (removing a little from one side will make the mount lopsided). Most faults are caused by a wobble or bulge in the cutting of the card or a dribble of dry glue.

If glass is the trouble, or if the picture is on a stretcher, then you will have to enlarge the rabbet of the frame by hand. Any trouble will

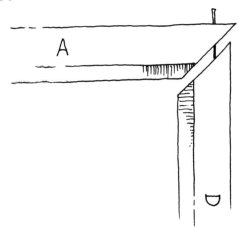

56 *The first location must be high*

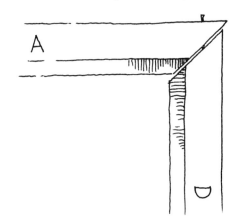

57 *As the pins are hammered in, the gap between the two pieces will begin to close*

MAKING THE FRAME

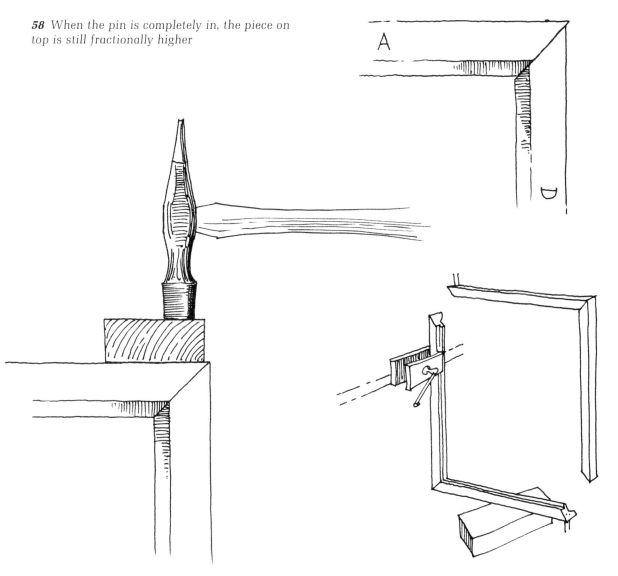

58 When the pin is completely in, the piece on top is still fractionally higher

59 The final tap on a protective block of wood will bring the two pieces perfectly in line

60 Make sure the lower part of C is supported when both L-pieces are brought together

only be slight (a bump on the glass); with a sharp blade in your knife and the frame face down on your working table the problem can easily be solved. Nonetheless, it is a nuisance when this happens and you will know that you need to be a little more generous when measuring next time.

Having too much clearance can in itself bring difficulties, although you can position the mount, glass or stretcher with pieces of mounting card used as packing. It may not seem to matter if a mount is a little smaller than the frame, but, if the opening has been carefully positioned in the whole mount, its quality can be spoilt if it drops in the frame, for more of the mount will be lost at the bottom and some gained at the top. To prevent this happening, slide in packing to bring the mount to the correct position. Once all the checking and fitting is confirmed, the treatment of the frame can be completed.

Choosing the right finish

Though the wood can be left as it is with merely some white wax furniture polish to seal the surface, the possibilities for the colours of your frame are endless. You must consider the picture, the mount, the wall colour and the whole environment. Light-coloured frames can look very handsome with dark mounts. Use emulsion paint – it dries to a good, even surface very quickly and white emulsion can be altered with any other water-thinned paint; poster colour is particularly useful.

Acrylic and polymer artists' paint are also excellent for frames. Trials for colours can be made using off-cuts, which as your collection grows, can be a very valuable reference (fig. 61). If the moulding is to have two colours, paint the paler one all over first. Give it a second coat and allow it to dry. The darker, second colour will then easily cover in one application. Where you require a colour change, I suggest that you do so between any moulding shapes. Let the change of shape or direction be the point of change in colour or texture. Some beautifully soft effects can be obtained by rubbing a very thin smear of the second colour onto the first. If you don't like the effect a rag with hot water will soon remove the paint. Another priming coat will remove any last trace.

Wood, when varnished, will tend to turn as much deeper and harsher colour. However, some synthetic varnishes may satisfactorily seal the surface without changing the colour too much and may be obtained in an egg-shell or matt finish as well as a high gloss.

Gold or silver paints will never look like gold or silver; they will look like paint, and some have a granular texture which is very noticeable when used over the total area of the frame. However, they are excellent for repairs and for lines or edges. Although excellent gold leaf framing is available from professional framers, the ancient and delicate craft of gilding is explained in connection with the repairing of old frames in Chapter 6.

Spray paint in small cans, made for car repairs, can be obtained in a wide range of colours. Best used on a prepared, primed surface, the colour should be built up in gradual stages to prevent running.

Assembling and finishing

When all is dry and the backing card is in place, small moulding pins or brads 20 mm ($\frac{3}{4}$ in.) long should be used to hold everything in place. To do this, lay the picture in its frame face down on the table, on top of newspaper or material to prevent its being scratched. Clamp a piece of wood with your vice or two metal clamps on the edge of the table (fig. 62). With the frame pressing against the block of wood, hammer in the pins towards yourself, sliding the hammer head on the backing card (fig. 63). (If you hammer in mid-air you may break the corners of the frame, or even the glass.) Broad water-based glued paper tape or masking tape should be applied to the joint between the frame and the backing card (fig. 64). This is not essential, but it prevents dust and small flies creeping in. Do not do this, however, if you are likely to change the picture often. Its removal can be a nuisance.

63 Working against the stop, the pins holding the work in the frame are gently tapped in. (They only need to penetrate 2 or 3 mm ($\frac{1}{8}$ in.)

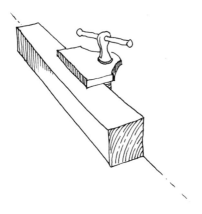

62 Wood clamped by a vice to form a stop

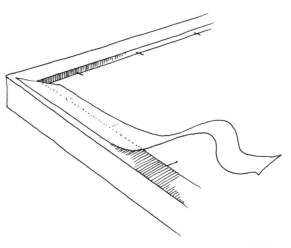

64 If the work is to be permanent tape should be applied to the back joint

MAKING THE FRAME

Alternative frames

Once you have grasped the sequence for making a frame and become adept in your judgements, you will probably want to try some variations.

A slip – a little inner edging – may be added to the main frame, making the overall dimensions wider and the opening smaller. This could be made of wood, stained, painted or covered with material. A frame could be filled with a sheet of hardboard, and on this a second, smaller-sectioned frame might be used for the actual framing of the picture. With wood sections available the variations are endless (fig. 65).

Aluminium can be bought in various lengths and sections, and it is a simple task to polish it with wire wool, kitchen scouring pads or scouring powder. Aluminium can be used as a batten for a canvas (fig. 66) or glued or screwed to the side of a frame. It is a strong but light

66 A strip of aluminium screwed to a painting's edge. (The holes should be countersunk)

MAKING THE FRAME

material, and a special hacksaw blade is needed to cut it. Figure 67 shows it being used to hold several separate stretchers, making up one larger painting. Small sections might be glued to the face of the frame to add a crisp, shiny line, but realize that as soon as your materials get more extensive, the price of your frame could quickly exceed the price of a bought one.

Professional framers and other shops do sell excellent frames, and I certainly use their services when I require larger sizes for oil paintings. Sometimes, although the section and scale may be excellent, the finish might not be quite right for the picture; the colour of some gold leaf may be over-harsh or it may be excessive. In this case the application of emulsion paint mixed to a sympathetic colour can be a most successful modification to some parts of the section (fig. 68). Even painting and wiping most of it off again with a rag or sponge, or dabbing with a paint-covered rag, can be effective (fig. 69). Once again, if possible, do a trial before committing yourself, and remember to wait for emulsion paint to dry before deciding if the colour is right; between wet and dry states there is quite a colour change. A strip of paper can be painted and propped up against the frame for consideration, but thin paint on reflective gold leaf won't produce the same colour.

Frame kits are available in a number of styles. The aluminium sections are very handsome and may be bought in 50 mm (2 in.) gradations, from about 200 mm (8 in.) to 1000 mm (36 in.). They are generally sold in a pack containing two sides, two packs making one

67 The strength of a metal strip allows several stretchers to be fixed together

frame (fig. 70). They are simple to assemble and are very strong at the corner joints. It is possible to dismantle these frames and swop sides, thus elements of two frames, one 300 mm (12 in.) × 600 mm (24 in.), the other 460 mm (18 in.) × 760 mm (30 in.) could be swopped to make a frame 300 mm (12 in.) × 460 mm (18 in.) and the other 600 mm (24 in.) × 760 mm (30 in.). As long as the same brand is used, infinite variations can be tried. With the addition of your own mounts, the resulting picture will look very fine. Because this type can be

68 *Colour samples painted on paper or tape indicate possible changes to a bought frame. Great care must be taken on gold leaf surfaces because any adhesion can remove the leaf*

disassembled and the picture removed, I find them ideal for use when picture sizes are similar and a need for constant changing exists. However, some exhibition organizers do not advise their use for they do find problems under certain conditions. When complying with submission instructions do note any limiting clauses.

Various frames for canvases are also available in kit form.

Chapter 5

FRAME VARIATIONS

There are several crafts which may require framing for their final presentation, but not necessarily the traditional methods used for drawings and paintings.

Pressed and dried flowers need a very gentle method of framing (fig. 71). They can be laid on a fine velvet-type material or any fabric with a yielding surface. If a softer base is needed, back the material with a thin sheet of soft foam plastic (the type used in forms of packing in industry). A firm backing of hardboard completes the 'sandwich' and allows a gentle pressure of the arrangement against the glass. Use a traditional wood frame with simple turnclips screwed into the top and bottom edges (fig. 72). Turnclips are preferable to pins or brads, which must be hammered in, for so fragile a subject; they also allow adjustments to be made to the composition more easily.

Three-dimensional pictures

If the flower arrangement is not entirely flat, a space will have to be created between the arrangement and the glass (fig. 73). Clean the glass and offer it into the chosen frame. The frame should have a sufficiently generous section at the back to allow for the following procedure.

Using either thin strips of balsa wood (available from modelmaking shops) or small blocks or strips of cork (table mats or floor tiles are excellent), glue these spacing pieces to the edge of the frame. They will, of course, hold the glass in place but must not be seen at the edge of the frame opening unless they form a very neatly applied, complete edge (fig. 73).

74 A collection of dried flowers need a space between glass and backing

72 The section of a frame with turn clips holding the backing

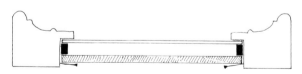

73 The section of a frame with spacing pieces introduced between glass and backing

The firm backing can then be covered with the chosen material and the dried flowers arranged and fixed, for the glass will not touch their surface or act as a pressure support in any way.

Samples of lace, embroidery and other low-relief objects might be presented in this way (figs 75 and 78).

If the chosen frame does not have a rabbet that allows a sufficient gap to be created, it is possible to take the backing piece across the back of the frame (fig. 76) rather than fitting it into the rabbet. Fix this with four roundhead screws.

Alternatively, the back could be extended by adding a rectangular section of wood (figs 77 and 79). Obviously, there must be a limit to the size, for the frame will be brought forward and this must not look uncomfortable. If a greater degree of edge concealment is required for, say, fixing stems, or if the frame is rather larger in size than the arrangement requires, a mount can be introduced into place immediately behind the glass (fig. 80). This may be fixed with small panel pins which, in turn, will keep the glass in place. Any spacing pieces would then be introduced after that.

Tapestry and embroidery

Tapestry and embroidery worked on a heavy backing should be presented with a flat surface and left on an embroidery frame, stretched on a solid sheet of block or chipboard, or stretched on an artist's canvas stretcher (fig. 81). When circular working stretchers are used in making, it is possible for you to put these

75 Samples of traditional lace

76 By taking the backing across the back of the frame, the greatest possible space is made available from the existing section

77 To gain more space than the actual frame section would provide, add an additional rectangle of wood

78 *A lace picture set well back from the inner edge of the frame*

FRAME VARIATIONS

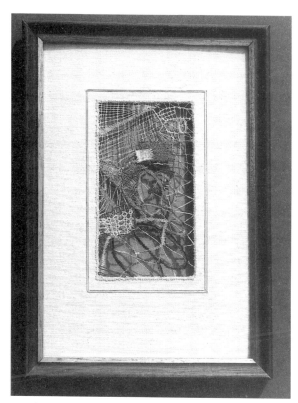

81a Embroidery on a traditional stretcher, viewed from the back. The ends could be stitched down tidily

79 A composition in modern lace – a good depth behind the design is required for shadows to be created. This particular work is not shown under glass

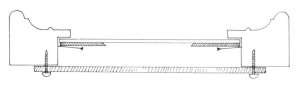

80 Placing a mount immediately behind the glass conceals more of the edges

81b The front view with some frame samples

directly into a frame; any screw-tightening device might require the frame back to be pared away slightly.

Canvas stretchers

Traditional canvas stretchers are ideal if used with care and are available in several widths, smaller for shorter lengths – i.e., approximately 45 mm ($1\frac{3}{4}$ in.) wide for lengths up to about 1 m (3 ft). Length sizes go up by 25 mm (1 in.). The pieces slot together at the corners (figs 82 and 83) and have wedges inserted on the inside of the rectangle (fig. 84) so that you can expand the overall size slightly to tighten the material fixed to the outer edges of the stretcher. Decide on the size you require your finished embroidery to be. If the outer edge is to be held in a frame, allow for about 5 mm ($\frac{1}{4}$ in.) to be covered.

With either pins or drawing pins, mark the corners of the embroidery so that, when turned over, the corner positions can be located. Lay the embroidery face down on a clean, firm work table. Assemble the stretcher into a rectangle – make sure it is precise by laying it on the corner of the table or by using a set square. Ensure that all four corners are tightly closed up. Do not put the wedges in at this stage. (Note that some types of stretcher do have a front and a back (fig. 85).)

Lay the stretcher down on the pack on the back of the embroidery, locating its position with the pins sticking through from the front. Bringing the surplus material over to the back and tensioning it lightly, hammer a tack into the middle of each side (fig. 86). Work outwards to each corner at approximately 50 mm (2 in.) intervals, stopping about 75 mm (3 in.) from

82 The end of one stretcher piece

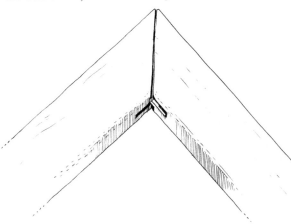

83 The corner of a stretcher

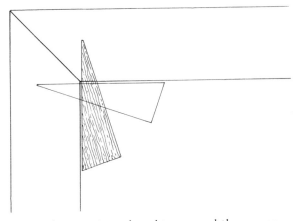

84 Wedges are introduced to expand the corner. Notice the tilt

FRAME VARIATIONS

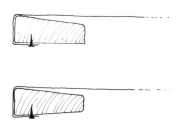

85 *Two of the most common stretcher sections. When buying two of a new size to add to some you have, take a sample to ensure that they are compatible*

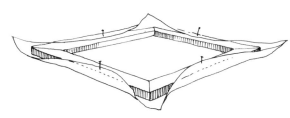

86 *Place one tack into the middle of each side*

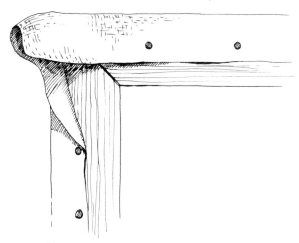

87 *Adding tacks; stop 75 mm (3 in.) from the corner*

each end (fig. 87). Make the first fold from the top of the corner (fig. 88), then make the second fold from the corner nearest the face of the embroidery (figs 89 and 90). Put two more tacks in to hold this corner fold in place (fig. 91).

Repeat on the other side. Turn the whole stretcher round and repeat with the other two corners. Ensure that the folds all bend left to right or right to left, for the folding does create an extra thickness and it will be neater and simpler if they are symmetrically done. Any surplus material can be left on but lightly tack it or stitch it across into a tidy arrangement. Position the eight wedges and tap in until the canvas has been tensioned. Do not over-expand the stretcher. It may look well hanging just like that, but if you wish to add a frame, measure the canvas carefully, for the thickness of the material can add a surprising amount.

If you use blockboard, slightly round the edges and corners with sandpaper in order to prevent a sharp edge damaging the material. Make the corner folds in exactly the same way, and secure them with a drawing pin. Lightly tension the material and hold in place by stitching across from the one side to the other.

If the embroidery is to be unglazed in the frame, I recommend lining the rabbet with thin strips of neutral-coloured felt, making sure it cannot be seen at the edge; this will provide a soft bed for the embroidery when it is located (fig. 92). Two or three long panel pins are enough to hold the whole stretcher in position (fig. 93). If, for protection from dust, glass is to be incorporated, clean it before inserting it into the frame, and then lighty glue a spacer slip of cork to the rabbet side. Alternatively, use tiny

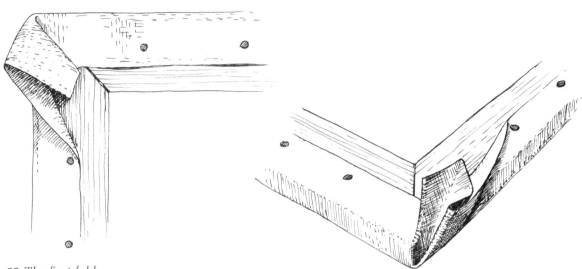

88 The first fold

90 The first and second folds

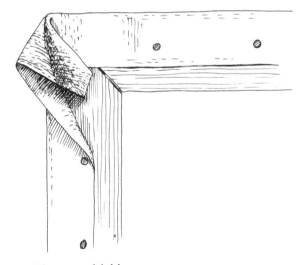

89 The second fold

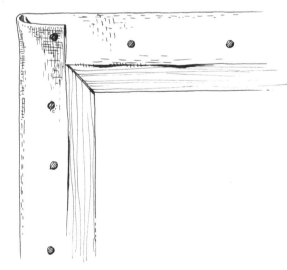

91 The corner fold tacked in place

panel pins to keep the spacer in place, but pins can rust and should be covered with tape if they are likely to come in contact with the face of the embroidery. When the stretcher is inserted the embroidery will then be just clear of the glass, and air can circulate.

Because of the thickness of the stretcher, the frame must, of course, have a deep rabbet – a small sectioned one suitable for watercolours will not be generous enough here.

92 *A felt strip making a soft bed for a framed embroidery*

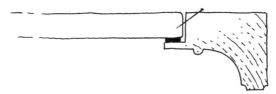

93 *Minimal fixing for a stretcher*

Box frames

An alternative to a deep-rabbetted frame is a shallow, glass-faced box, which also allows you to see the whole embroidery (fig. 94). Objects in show cases always seem to have a particularly precious quality. The single object behind glass in a shop window has a similar focus given to it. Be quite generous when calculating the size: the space inside the box is more crucial than the overall outside dimensions. The proportions of a card mount are appropriate, but the depth will, of course, relate to the object being presented.

Cut the mitres of the box sides, and then assemble the sides, checking the angles with a set square. Lay the rectangle on a piece of plywood or chipboard, mark on it the inside of the box walls and cut to size. This should fit snugly. If the base is thick ply, screw directly through the top and bottom walls into the thickness of the plywood (fig. 95). If the plywood is too thin to take a screw, edge the plywood at the back with a 5 mm ($\frac{1}{4}$ in.) square section of wood and screw into this (fig. 96). Take account of the loss in depth on the inside of the box.

The picture will be fixed to the removable plywood back so the glass can be fixed permanently. Cut a piece large enough to lie half across the front face of the side walls and then, with a very thin piece of wood, just thicker than the glass, mitred at the corners, complete the surface to the outside edge of the wall. Alternatively use cork sheet, thick mounting card or an aluminium strip in place of wood. This material is then covered by a thin batten of wood, again mitred at the corners,

94 *A glass-faced box arranged to reveal its elements*

which will trap the glass (fig. 97). The width of this batten should be equal to or slightly wider than the width of the wall of the box. Glue the strip at the side of the glass to the wall, lay the glass in the created rabbet, and glue the top batten on top.

If the rabbet strip is metal it can be drilled first and the top batten fixed with the finest moulding pins, possibly brass.

Beware of glues or wood fillers which seal the surface. If subsequently varnished, the change in absorbency will result in unsightly colour variations.

This box can be made in a variety of ways, and I realize that carpenters would happily rabbet the top edge of the wall; however, the effect would be similar and the method described above might be easier for someone less experienced.

A very old canvas, or a painting on a wood panel, possibly a damaged painting that would present problems for normal frames and pro-

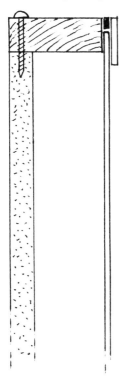

95 The section of a glass-faced box, with the back fixed by screwing through the side

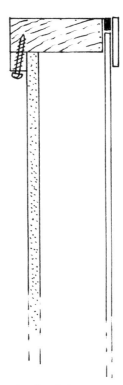

96 An alternative back fixing

97 *The corner of the box with a sample of glass
and its location*

tection, might be particularly suited to a box of this type. To place a canvas in such a box, simply stick two blocks of wood so that the stretcher can hang on the top of them (fig. 98). Screws through the backing plywood might fix a less precious painting (fig. 99). Nylon-hooked tape, which dressmakers use, could also provide the solution, one side being fixed to the back of the article and the other to the back panel (fig. 100).

'No-frame' frames

Some styles of interior design emphasize function and clearness of structure. A support for a drawing which has virtually no frame can look very crisp and clean. The basis is a backing board of plywood, chipboard or blockboard, about 20 mm (¾ in.) thick. Pre-cut blockboard has good crisp edges because it is cut with a circular saw. If you wish to cut the material at home, clamp it to a work-table or similar firm support so that it does not swivel as you saw.

Cut a sheet of glass to exactly the same size, but bevell the sharp edges. You can do this by carefully smoothing the sharp edge with a coarse emery paper or a fine stone used for sharpening tools. Fix the glass with small metal or plastic L-shaped clips which screw into the side of the backing board (fig. 101). This sort of frame is good for work on paper where no mount is needed, or where a paper mount is used (fig. 102). It is a useful frame for a student, for the work can be changed quickly. The screws fixing the clips will have to be repositioned if the thickness of the mounted material is altered. It is not a very safe method

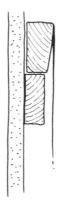

98 Support for a stretcher provided by blocks of wood

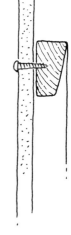

99 The stretcher screwed through from the back

100 Nylon-hooked tape, half fixed to the backing, half to the stretcher

101 Glass held to the backing board by metal clips

102 A 'no-frame' frame

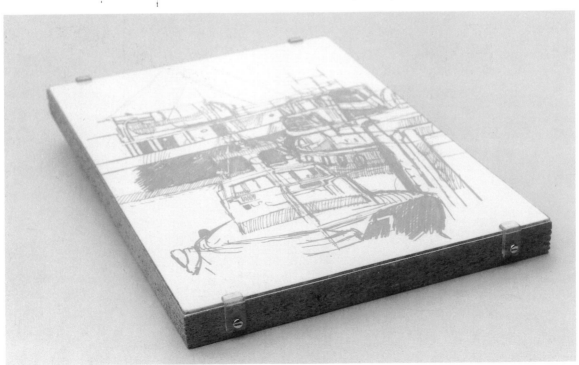

FRAME VARIATIONS

of framing for work which has to be transported, for the glass can be broken easily. A less vulnerable version can be made which has a small batten of wood added round the outside edge of the board to act as a buffer (fig. 103).

A clear, synthetic material – acetate sheet sometimes prepared for domestic glazing – might be used in some of the frames, although some types scratch easily, even by dusting. The advantage is that the material is light and simple to cut, and if you use an appropriate glue it is possible to create a variation on the box idea.

Synthetic material is also useful if you want a clear backing (perhaps because there are notes or another picture on the reverse). Use two sheets of clear material to sandwich the paper and hold them together with the plastic edging used for keeping documents together. A base block would allow the whole to stand upright, allowing both sides to be visible (fig. 104). But there does come a moment when one really leaves the world of the frame maker and becomes a display maker; whatever is created, it should be the object which claims the attention, and the support should not detract from that.

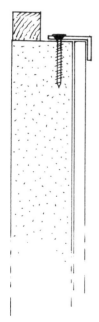

103 An additional buffer of wood giving some protection to the glass

104 Two clear panels enabling both sides of a work to be seen

Chapter 6

OLD FRAMES

Do nothing to an old frame until you are certain that it has no antique value (fig. 105). Your nearest antique furniture shop will guide you, or ask their advice as to whom you can consult. Once you are sure you are not devaluing the frame, you can try treating it by one of these methods.

Gold frames

Gold frames – frames covered with a white plaster-like ground called gesso, then a layer of red bole, and finally gold leaf on top – should never be washed, wiped or rubbed harshly. If you do so, you will quickly remove the gold leaf and expose the red bole. Further rubbing will then lay bare the white ground (fig. 106).

After a gentle general clean up with white spirit – excellent because it does not dissolve water-based glue and does not leave any sticky deposit – replace any lost moulding with car-body filler (fig. 107); there is a type described as *elastic* which is easily cut and sanded even when dry. A complicated piece could be cast with reusable rubber mould material – particularly useful where a repeat pattern is involved.

At this stage you must choose between a simple finish using gold paint, or the more complex process using gold leaf. If you choose paint, match the gold to the nearest pot of gold paint you are able to buy – there are a lot of shades – but only paint your repairs and spot any chips. Proprietary brands of gold preparations in paste form are available for touching up. Gold marker pens might also serve for small touches, but colour-matching will be crucial to achieve a successful appearance.

If the frame is a particularly fine one and is in a relatively good state despite a few pieces of broken moulding, then it could be worth repairing it and adding gold leaf. It can be expensive, however; a book of gold leaf containing 25 sheets, each about 85 mm ($3\frac{1}{4}$ in.) square, will probably cost more than a simple, bought frame, but the quality of the repaired frame will be restored. There are also less expensive gold-coloured metal leaf books which produce a quality near to real gold leaf.

Gilding

The gilder's craft is a very ancient one and, like many other crafts, is simple in many ways, yet requiring deft skills acquired only with practice and by observation of others at work. However, although a beginner may be clumsy when compared with an expert, you can still succeed to the degree required. You will need:

- gold (or metal and silver is available as well) leaf
- gilder's cushion
- gilder's knife
- gilder's tip
- rabbit-skin glue
- methylated spirits
- red bole
- whiting (chalk)
- agate burnisher
- double boiler (or two saucepans, one of which will fit inside the other)
- spirit (camping) stove
- palette knife
- cotton wool

106 A frame which has lost its gold leaf on the left hand side and which also has chips and flakes needing attention

107 Car-body filler is ideal for replacing small pieces of moulding

The gilder's cushion or board (150 mm (6 in.) × 200 mm (8 in.)) is made from a piece of card covered on the top side with a thin pad of cotton wool, and the whole then covered by a soft piece of calf leather – suede-side up. A finger loop for holding it is made at the back (fig. 108). The knife is a broad-bladed, spatula-type tool; a kitchen spatula or broad-blade knife might serve (fig. 109). It is used for cutting and moving leaf. The gilder's tip is a broad brush; the hairs are set between two rectangles of card which make the handle (fig. 110).

Having repaired the basic shape of the moulding, you need to cover the surface with an ultra-smooth coating – this is called gesso ground. Much has been written on this subject and it makes fascinating reading. However, I shall describe two processes, which I hope will not offend professional gilders, but which are simple to follow and, what is important for the amateur, they work!

Method 1: Water gilding

Soak two tablespoonfuls of rabbit-skin glue (in granulated form) or one-quarter of a sheet in water overnight. The glue will take up its own weight of water and swell to jelly-like lumps. (I always seem to prepare more than I need but as you cannot speed the soaking, if you don't have enough when you come to start, you're held up.)

A double-boiler – a container which sits in a larger second container holding water – is brought to a state where the heating water in the lower container is just on boiling. The glue is then diluted by about fifteen parts water to one of glue – this is very approximate! Warm water can be used which will speed up the

108 The back of the gilder's cushion showing the finger loop

109 A gilder's knife, modified in this case from a spatula

110 A gilder's tip – a card handled brush

111 Gilding implements (from top, clockwise): a
glue pot, a methylated spirit stove, a gilder's
knife, a gilder's tip and a book of leaf resting on a
gilder's cushion, a metal plate for mixing, an
agate burnisher and a palette knife

process of melting the lumps. The test for the glue is that finger and thumb should just stick together when wetted with the glue and blown dry. Of course, the skin will not completely stick, but the adhesion will be felt. The look of the glue when cool and set will be like a table jelly. This thin glue is the medium and should be kept warm in the top of the boiler.

Pour a small pile of whiting (chalk) on a piece of glass or other flat surface. With a palette knife, mix a little glue into the powder until a very smooth cream results. If this thickens transfer it to a saucer and place over the steaming water in the boiler to make it more liquid again. Lay this preparation onto the necessary parts of the frame with a soft brush and allow it to dry. Sand this coating with extremely fine sandpaper and repeat the process until the smoothest surface possible is obtained.

Red bole (a sort of red earth colour) is optional but it adds a good underlying tone; put it on a clean surface and, with a little of the warm glue, grind it into a thin cream with the palette knife. (This can also be bought in paste form, ready to mix with the glue.) Paint the red bole over the dry, white areas of the gesso and allow it to dry (fig. 112). Next, mix about one part methylated spirits to four parts thin, warm glue in a small jar. This should be put ready to hand with a soft watercolour-type brush close by for the application.

Ensure all doors and windows are closed, and then carefully open the tissue-paper-leaved book containing the gold leaf – any draught will cause havoc! Holding the gilder's cushion in one hand and the gilder's knife in

the other, slide the blade under one sheet of leaf and lift it onto the cushion (fig. 113). Straighten it out with the help of the knife and then cut it by drawing the knife gently across the surface (fig. 114). Be generous with the piece you cut so that it more than covers the patch you are restoring.

Damp the area of bole to be covered with the glue/meths liquid. Give a slight static charge to the gilder's tip by drawing it across your face or hair, and then touch the piece of leaf with it. It will adhere sufficiently to allow you to remove the piece of gold leaf from the cushion and lay it on the frame (fig. 115). Very lightly, press the leaf down with a pad of cotton wool. Continue laying leaf on all areas and leave the frame to dry overnight.

112 Red bole being applied

113 Lifting one sheet of leaf

115 Lifting the gold leaf with the gilder's tip

114 Cutting the sheet

116 An application of leaf being burnished

Next day, lightly brush away unstuck pieces of leaf and, with an agate burnisher, gently bring a smooth firm pressure to bear on the newly applied leaf, rubbing the burnisher backwards and forwards (fig. 116). The gold will obtain a high lustre.

Method 2: Oil gilding

Oil gilding requires the same, smooth gesso surface and the red bole gives a good rich tone, although, again, this is optional. Once you have applied the gesso to the damaged areas, seal the surface with shellac. Then apply Japan Gold Size, which can be obtained ready-made in the bottle from art suppliers. It is a special mixture of copal varnish and dryers and is applied to the shellac and allowed to dry until it is just tacky enough to receive the gold leaf.

Shellac can also be applied to paper or any other absorbent surface, followed by the Japan Gold Size, before the gold leaf is applied. The limitation of oil gilding is that the leaf cannot be burnished.

If the gold leaf is in a bad state and the frame is already covered with gold paint, you may want to paint the whole or part of the frame (fig. 117). For a complete strip down, leave the frame out to weather – or soak it in water – so that the plaster gradually drops off. The resulting basic wood frame can then be given a scrub and a wax polish.

Decreasing the frame size

If the frame that you want to cut down is covered in any form of ground or plaster, the ground material will chip and fail to give a crisp, clean joint when re-cut. In some cases it may be very hard and will stand proud of the freshly cut mitred wood beneath. However, re-mitring most small, sectional frames presents no great problem (fig. 118). Check on the capacity of your mitre box or cutting device – many old oil painting frames, even with their plaster mouldings removed, are quite wide and will not fit. If a frame is to be reduced in size, and the existing mitres are sound, consider cutting only two diagonally opposite corners. Rather like cutting a cake, a very thin slice is much more difficult than a good hunk.

If you are trying to remove only 10 mm ($\frac{3}{8}$ in.), you may have to cut through nails; for this you will need a fine, long hacksaw which will be guided by your mitre box slots. If more can be removed to provide you with a frame of your required size, cut the frame either side of one corner with a saw, and repeat these two cuts at the corner diagonally opposite. The two L-shaped pieces can now be re-mitred, although the weight of the additional side attached may require an extra helping hand to support it, while you concentrate on maintaining the position of the frame to cut the mitre.

It is easiest of all to detach all the corners, re-mitre and completely reassemble the pieces. The rejoining presents no special problem, except that the wood may be very hard and reject soft moulding pins or split when you try to put them in; it is a good idea, therefore, to drill two, fine holes first. The points of the nails pushed through them should be used to guide any holes made in the other receiving half of the mitre.

If you have problems with inserting pins in re-mitred wood use clamps, or piles of heavy

117 A frame with paint applied in different ways:
the top – brushed on, highlighting the tops of the
moulding; the top right hand side – total paint
cover; the bottom right – total paint cover, but
with the paint wiped off the tops of the moulding

books or bricks to hold the frame in place with glue alone in the joint. Wood glues or impact glues are good (i.e., those that are applied to both surfaces and after a short time the two surfaces can be brought together). Any old holes can easily be filled with a wood or plastic filler and touched in with an appropriate spot of paint. Wax shoe polish is excellent for staining and filling wood – force it well into the joint (this is where the whiskers left on cut wood can help) and rub off the surplus with a rag. Even coloured pencils are useful for toning in repairs. However, do not get over-concerned about variations. When the frame is finally on the wall, it is the total effect which will be noticed, not the little blemish.

118 *A damaged frame re-mitred to be made up again to a smaller size*

Glazing

Many older oil paintings were framed with exceedingly thick, heavy glass. Most oil paintings look better without this, for the quality of the paint surface can be appreciated and there are fewer disturbing reflections. Oil paint is quite durable and, if varnished, may be carefully dusted, then cleaned with a damp sponge. Proprietary brands of cleaner fluid are available from art suppliers. However, at all stages, great care must be taken. *When in doubt, don't!*

Airborn dust and grease can accumulate very quickly and, since paper is absorbent, watercolours and drawings should be covered by glass. The most straightforward and economical solution is a visit to your local glass merchants. They will help you decide what weight/thickness you require; for a watercolour a thickness of 2–3 mm ($\frac{1}{8}$ in.) will be about right. Do give them the exact size (3 mm ($\frac{1}{8}$ in.) less than the opening).

Personally, I do not like non-reflective glass – the slightly textured surface is often more obvious than the reflections. The whole quality of drawings, watercolours and prints is the surface and you need actually to see every fine mark and change.

If you have a large sheet of glass and require a smaller piece, you will need a glass cutter, a straight-edge, a T square or a set square, and a piece of felt or other material on which you can lay your glass. Mark out the size with care and decide which side of the line you are going to score. A special pencil for marking glass is useful, but a fibre-tip pen will make a perfectly clear line (though it is instantly smudged). All

lines must be taken right through from edge to edge of the sheet of glass. You cannot cut out a corner, leaving an L-shaped piece over, as you can with a sheet of mounting card.

With your straight-edge as a guide, press the glass cutter firmly onto the glass surface (fig. 119). You will feel it bite into the glass and while you move the cutter you must maintain a downward pressure. Ensure you have incised the line right to the edges, both at the start and finish. Slide your straight-edge under the glass to the immediate left of the incision and press the right-hand side down – the glass should snap cleanly (fig. 120). There is a knack, and

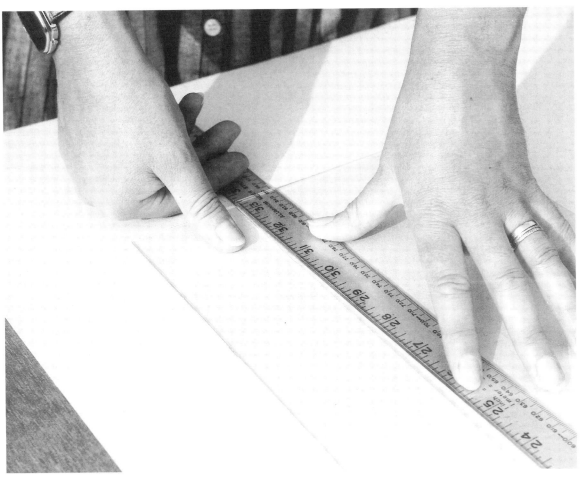

though, of course, glass can cut you, do not be frightened of the material; a firmness of handling is required. However, you may prefer to get an experienced cutter to provide your glass, and if you collect it, do go prepared with material or corrugated cardboard for wrapping. If you put more than one sheet in the boot of your car, make certain that they cannot slide sideways on one another – a likely happening when you turn corners. In the house, glass is best stacked upright against a wall, and obviously well out of the way of passing feet, children and the family pet!

Chapter 7

DISPLAY

Where to hang your frame

Cart before the horse, or horse before the cart? Do you have a wall and find a picture which suits it, or do you have a picture for which you have to find a suitable wall? There are some basic points to consider and some basic do's and don'ts, but the ultimate choice is yours.

When you are considering the redecoration of a room or house, do not just think of walls and curtains. If you have pictures, plan how the wall colours will show them to best advantage, and just thinking often is not enough. Samples of colours on a paint manufacturer's card look so completely different when seen over a large area. It is worth trying samples, even if you feel confident. Buy the smallest tin of your chosen wall colour and paint a piece of card or hardboard. Prop it up in your room and live with it for some days; prop up your pictures alongside it and look at them at different times of the day. Try samples of wallpaper in the same way (fig. 121). This sort of trying out – not just thinking out – is essential.

Attractive little pictures may look very lost on a large expanse of wall, and larger pictures may dwarf a room; however, do not be put off by big pictures – the idea that you have to stand back from them is not always true. Sometimes a large picture, say 1.2 × 1.5 m (4 × 5 ft), can hang very well in a small sitting room, and can be very effective when viewed through the open door of a neighbouring room (fig. 122). Therefore, don't rule out any sites in your house without experimenting, and do find a place where a cluster of small works can accumulate (fig. 123).

A common fault is that of hanging pictures too high on a wall. Many can be looked into with a lot of pleasure, so their centres should rarely be above eye level. Perhaps some thought should also be given to picture heights from a sitting position. There are hazards, of course; the pine chest has an added importance with paintings hanging above it – fine, that is, until you want to open it and the lid bangs on the pictures (fig. 124)!

People, referring to pictures they dislike, laugh and talk of hanging them in the loo – but why not have a print or map there? People often reject bathrooms and kitchens because of damage caused by steam or grease, but non-precious pictures can always be hung and then should any staining or marks occur, renewed or replaced like the paintwork (fig. 125).

Radiators and various forms of heating appliance can do damage, for though the warmth itself may not harm a work, the dirt carried in the upward current of air builds up on picture surfaces – and this applies to the cleanest of houses. Here one should choose a glazed work, with a frame, which can be easily wiped clean.

123 A trio of drawings with room for more to be added

124 *You need to be careful when hanging pictures. The lid of this pine chest, for example, will touch the pictures hanging above it when opened*

Hanging pictures

To hang a picture, one of the most valuable and simple aids is the masonry nail (fig. 126). This specially hardened, thickish nail can be bought in various lengths and can be driven into most brick walls. It should always bite into the main structure of the wall, for the surface plaster or facing may not take much load.

126 A masonry nail

Man-made types of compressed board-covered wall will receive any sort of nail, preferably one with a head, but wood coverings (like panelling) are best drilled first to prevent a possible split, and a screw used instead. Many houses may be built with the same materials throughout, so trials in one place could guide you elsewhere, but when alterations have taken place, you may encounter a considerable variety of textures. If you have a very hard wall you may need to drill a hole with a masonry bit and put a special plug into the hole before inserting the screw (fig. 127).

127 A wall plug and a fast screw

An alternative for hanging very heavy objects is a masonry bolt which screws into an expandable casing (fig. 128). The whole unit is pushed into the hole, of an exact matching size, and the bolt is then carefully removed; the object or a metal hook is offered into place and the bolt replaced. As the bolt is tightened, the casing in the wall expands and tightens in the hole.

128 A masonry bolt for heavy fixing (also known as a raw bolt)

Should you discover that the wall is hollow, then use the special type of fixing available (fig. 129).

It is important to decide how you want to attach your picture to the wall as this will dictate the fixings on the back of the frame.

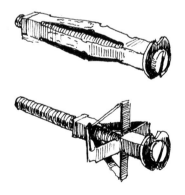

129 A hollow wall fixing, shown before use and once inside the cavity

Most pictures can be satisfactorily hung by screwing in two small eyes, about 75 mm (3 in.) from the top of the picture. Between these two points some thin, 20 gauge, galvanized wire is stretched. The wire, when taking the weight of the picture, will pull upwards a little. It should be sufficiently tensioned so as not to get nearer than about 40 mm ($1\frac{1}{2}$ in.) from the top of the picture (fig. 130). The distance from the wire to the top of the picture can be marked on an odd piece of card (fig. 131). Find the middle of the top of the picture and mark it in some impermanent way. Then hold your picture up in its chosen position, make the tiniest dot on the wall with a hard pencil, exactly at the centre top, and remove the picture. The distance marked on the card now indicates the distance at which the nail must be placed below the mark on the wall (fig. 132).

Then drive the masonry nail into the wall at a slight angle. Its head should be left about 10 mm ($\frac{3}{8}$ in.) from the wall surface. Hook the picture onto the nail and adjust it to a horizontal position. The downward slope of the nail will carry the wire close to the wall and give the greatest strength (fig. 133). You can see no sign of the fixing from the front of the picture with this basic method. Do not use string instead of wire for hanging; in time it will rot and your picture will fall. There is an exception to this – thick, smooth string is ideal for use in a temporary exhibition. Nails can be put into a wall quickly, heights can be judged by eye, and pictures moved up or down by slipping the single knot in the string through the screw eye (figs 134–7).

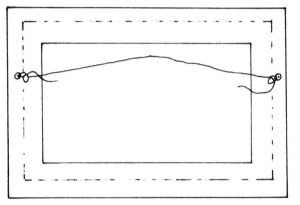

130 *The best place for a picture wire*

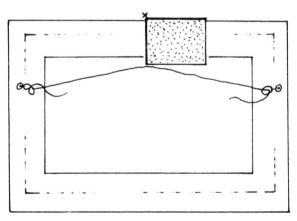

131 *The distance from the wire to the top of the picture being measured*

132 *The measure used to site the wall nail*

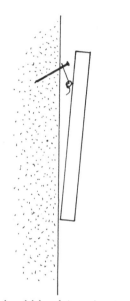

133 The nail should be driven in at a downward slope

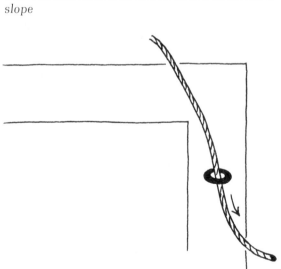

134 Thread the string from the top downwards

135 Loop it round

136 Bring it back through the loop

137 Tighten or untighten to shift the position

This basic method may necessitate modifications if you use very thin frames – most likely bought frames with attractive moulding or colour, but little *twist* strength. This twist is caused by the pull of the wire across the back of the picture, and, when the rabbet depth is great, this levering action of the wire on the screw eye can distort the side members. You can prevent this by: hanging each side separately with a single wire going up vertically to its own wall fixing; using a backing piece, such as hardboard, with a bar of wood glued to it, the screw eyes being screwed into the wood; or by using a blockboard backing, which can be screwed into directly.

Professional framers usually provide little screw eyes with a ring attached. These are not generally very satisfactory when used with wire, for the wire moves in the eye. They are best used by hanging on brass hooks that are fixed with hardened pins. However, the pins go into the wall rather awkwardly, too close to the edge of the picture. It is not easy to correct alignment, and if you wish to move the picture, the mark on the wall can be seen more clearly than that left by a single nail.

Heavy pictures

If the picture is heavy and the wall of questionable condition, and/or if the picture is to lie absolutely flat against the wall, then mirror plates can be used. These are made of brass or other metal and are of a stubby T-shape (fig. 138). Two holes lie in the crosspiece which take two fixing screws into the picture or object framed and will be countersunk on that side. The third hole lies in the rounded stem which takes the fixing into the wall, and is countersunk on the opposite side. When using mirror plates, notice which side has the bevelled, countersunk hole (taking the neck shape of the screw) and use accordingly. Two or four of these plates will produce a very firm fixing. Place them at the top and bottom of the frame where they will be seen least. When in place, the part of the plate which is seen can be painted to match the wall; matt paint used by model makers, is likely to be most suitable.

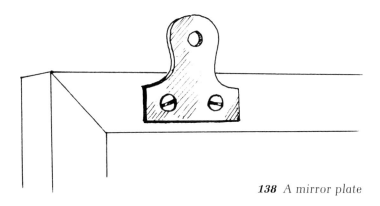

138 A mirror plate

Fixings for canvas

Two masonry nails spaced about 500 mm (20 in.) apart, on a well-chosen level, will provide perfectly adequate fixing for a canvas alone (or lightly battened) and have the added advantage that the work can be lifted off the nails (which stand out from the wall only 10 mm ($\frac{3}{8}$ in.)) and replaced with another. Since stretchers are made to a standard depth (most painters will find an advantage in working with either a 45 mm ($1\frac{3}{4}$ in.) or 50 mm (2 in.) standard) even a painting with dimensions of 1.2 m (4 ft) can be hung on the two nails, as long as they were originally placed on a central axis of the wall, allowing picture space at both sides. N.B. Since the stretcher is hanging on the nail, there is no protection between the nail head and the canvas, so the length of the protruding nails must be checked very carefully to ensure they will not puncture the canvas (fig. 139).

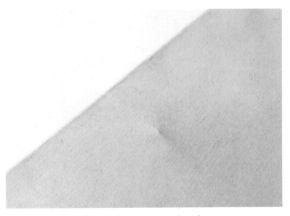

139 *A wall nail left too long – the damage to a canvas can be serious*

As an artist, paintings and drawings in my house never seem to stay in one place for very long, so I choose to use secure but the most versatile fixings, allowing groups to be adjusted and added to, and pictures to replace one another as they are removed from the easel. Very often, the masonry nail seems to fit the bill satisfactorily.

Hanging groups of pictures

Group hanging can, at first glance, look complicated, but it is not really, if you apply one or two rules. The *lane* system gives a unity to any group and allows you to make additions to the group without repositioning the other pictures. Two pictures would hardly qualify as a group, but the lane, or gap, between them is important if they are to be viewed as two pictures together, and not just two pictures hanging on the same wall (fig. 140).

Obviously, it is a question of actual size and the lightness or darkness in appearance of the pictures which dictates whether or not they seem to belong together. A rough guide would be to space them the width of the mount apart – i.e., if a picture has a 100 mm (4 in.) mount, then the wall space between frames (either side by side or one above the other) would be 100 mm (4 in.). If in doubt, keep the frames closer to rather than further away from one another. There is a sort of visual magnetic pull which will exist between the pictures – too close and they will disturb one another; too far away and they begin to look separate. If the pictures are oil paintings, then the gap could well be the width of the frame section or 100 mm (4 in.), whichever is the larger.

Clear an area on the floor and experiment with the picture positions. There are three possible side-by-side lining up methods for two pictures of different sizes: first, you can line up the middle of each picture (fig. 141); secondly, you can line up the tops (fig. 142); thirdly, you can line up the bottoms (fig. 143). For two pictures of similar size, line up the middles; if there is a considerable difference in size, say by one-third, then to line up the bottoms will give the calmest relationship.

Three pictures of roughly the same size are best in a row, with their middles lined up (fig. 144); if one is larger, line up the tops (fig. 145) or bottoms (fig. 146). If a group of three is made of two small, but similar sized pictures, and a third twice the size of the others, place the two smaller ones above the larger (fig. 147). (A good rule here is that pictures smaller or lighter in appearance should always be above another work.) The lane between the two smaller ones should be the same as the lane between the two smaller ones and the larger one.

With four pictures or more, the lane method is most useful. However varied the pictures are in size, it preserves a degree of organization whilst giving you the freedom to put the pictures in any order. Try out your four arrangement on the floor. Choose the first, place number two by its left side with the 100 mm (4 in.) lane separating them and the tops aligned. Place number three above two so that their right-hand edges line up, and place number four a lane width away and with its left-hand edge lining up with the left-hand edge of picture number one (fig. 148). Of course, you can try changing the positions of pictures, but

the principle remains the same – the cross-lane maintains order. If the four pictures are the same size, I suggest you use this system rather than trying to place them in a random way (fig. 149).

For most domestic wall areas, a basic two-row system is convenient, but if the wall area upwards and downwards allows, you can add more rows (fig. 150). Start with your favourite, laying it on the ground. To its left, lay a second picture and line up the tops; to the right, lay a third and line up the tops; lay a fourth to the right again. Now work on the second row above the first, and, with picture number five, place it partly above one and partly above three; then, add six to the left and seven to the right. If there is room, eight, nine and ten could be added in the gaps above and below; however, those above five, six and seven, must line up with one of the boundaries below them. Line eight up with five (the lane to the right is maintained). Below, line nine up with the left of three, and ten with the left of the favourite first. Those added into the holes should never be centred to those above, or below, or left or right, but lined up one side or the other to maintain the lane on that side. If a circular or oval frame is part of the group, line it up as if a rectangle has been constructed, the boundary touching the oval, and it will obey the same rules.

There may be a room which demands a horizontal line at the base of the group – for example, where the wall surface changes from plaster to panelling (fig. 151). In this case, position the first row with the bottoms in line. Build upwards, possibly maintaining one or two main lines vertically.

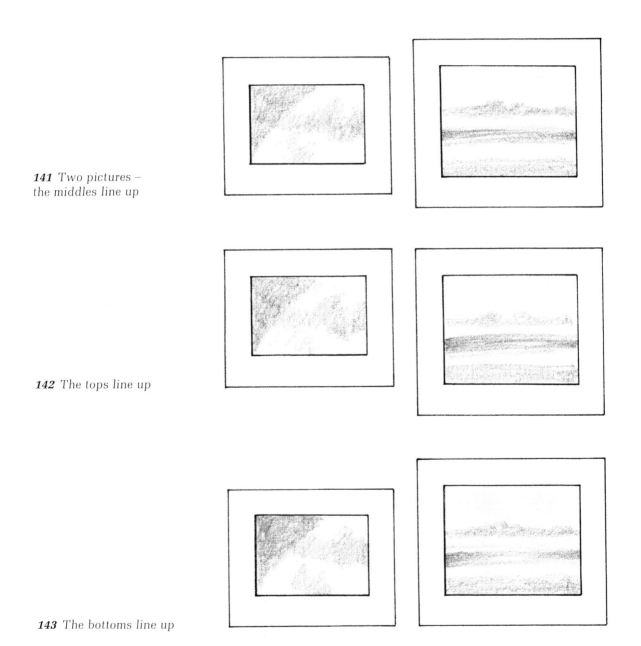

141 Two pictures –
the middles line up

142 The tops line up

143 The bottoms line up

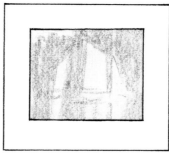
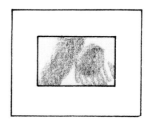

144 *Three pictures near the same size with the middles lined up*

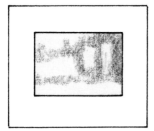

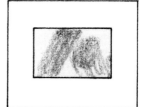

145 *Three pictures, one of which is large, shown with the tops lined up*

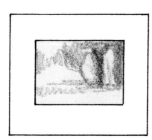

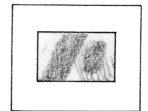

146 *The same group shown with the bottoms lined up*

147 Two smaller pictures are likely to be more
comfortable above a larger work

148 An arrangement of four various-sized pictures

Groups on the walls of a staircase can be very pleasant (fig. 152). Frequently, a staircase is a difficult place to reach to hang one big painting, so a collection, perhaps family photographs, is a simple solution. Here the group can grow upwards and sideways by maintaining the lanes and lining up at least one side each time. The group will look so much more attractive than the regular beat of one frame, one frame, one frame – slightly reminiscent of advertisements on the walls of Underground escalators (fig. 153).

Lighting

Watercolours can be adversely affected by strong, direct sunlight, so avoid positions where this can occur for prolonged periods, although reflections in glass can bring an added sparkle to a wall (fig. 154). However, it is when daylight fades that special thought should be given to illumination.

Lighting can affect the whole atmosphere of a room and, all too often, lighting pictures is not given enough importance. Purpose-made picture lights sometimes distract the eye from the actual picture – often, a spotlight is preferable. These can be very small and located on the ceiling or the ends of pelmets, freestanding or standing on tables or chests, possibly partly hidden by flowers or other objects. Spotlights, pointing upwards, light pictures very effectively with the minimum of

153 *A narrow staircase given interest by a collection of pictures*

installation and expense (fig. 155). Of course, if you can plan lighting when wiring the house, you may be able to use some of the track systems. The track is a long metal slot which carries the electrical current. Special lamps are locked into the slot anywhere along the length of the track. You can often see such a system in shop windows.

Some people do not like the rawness of spotlights, even if they are covered by a casing. If you prefer them, table lamps, hanging lamps and standard or standing lamps can be carefully positioned to throw a good light on the pictures. These are not always ideal to show the real quality of pictures, but pleasantly atmospheric.

Care of pictures

Pictures need very little care once they are hung. Glass should be kept clean, but take care not to rub the frame, for any surface can be removed over a period of time by abrasive rubbing. Use a dry, light cloth for dusting the frame.

Keep room temperature as constant as possible. Oil paintings are particularly vulnerable to temperature and humidity changes. Canvas can become floppy and wrinkled (fig. 156); if this happens do nothing to the canvas if the reason for change is obvious and temporary. If, however, over a period of stable house and climatic conditions, the slackness remains, take the picture down and lightly tap the corner wedges further in to expand the wooden stretcher slightly; this, in turn, will tighten the canvas (fig. 157). On no account over-tighten the canvas; old material can split.

156 Wrinkles in an untensioned canvas

157 The back of a canvas and stretcher with the wedges opening up the corner

A new painting needs no varnish – oil paint takes months to dry fully and, under normal conditions, will not be harmed. The lightest damp, soft cloth will remove any film of dirt.

If the painting dries with an uneven surface, glossy in some places, matt in others, owing to variations in the oil content of the paint, a thin coat of a synthetic varnish produced by a reputable artists' material manufacturer should be applied to the whole surface. Some old varnishes turned yellow and, what was worse, could not be removed. Modern varnishes can be removed simply with white spirit (double-rectified paraffin – sometimes called turpentine substitute). To varnish a picture first remove it from its frame. I must emphasize that, although some artwork is quite robust and with care will not be harmed, much could be irrevocably damaged by harsh cleaning or handling. If you have any pictures about which you know no definite facts, seek specialist advice first. The sort of people to ask will vary with the type of work, but most museums and public art galleries have experienced staff, and allocate certain times for dealing with such enquiries.

Glossary

Acid-free materials Mounting cards and papers which, by their composition, will not discolour or develop spots as they age. Different qualities are available

Agate burnisher A tool consisting of a wooden handle and a smooth shaped agate stone set at its tip. It is used to bring a shine to gold leaf laid on a gesso ground

Batten A thin, flat strip round the edge of a painting – generally made of wood or metal

Bit A metal rod spirally grooved and with a cutting tip. A great range of sizes is available

Bole An earth pigment containing red iron oxide which when mixed with water-based glue is used to give a ground colour prior to applying gold leaf

Bradawl A metal point with a handle for making an introductory hole in wood

Canvas Linen canvas is the best; cotton and jute are less durable but perfectly adequate

Chalk Prepared calcium carbonate. Natural chalk is called whiting and is obtainable from chemists in powder form. Other fine white pigment can be added to chalk to improve covering power, e.g., titanium dioxide

Cutting mats Proprietary brands of a special plastic sheet are available for cutting card on. However, off-cuts of mounting card are perfectly suitable

Drill The most useful hand-operated drill is the wheel brace, having a side wheel geared to the turning head. The cutting piece is called a bit

Dry mounting paper A thin paper coated on both sides with a heat-softened glue. It is used by photographers for mounting photographs onto card. A proprietary brand of glue in a pressurized container is available which performs a similar function

Emulsion paint A synthetic paint which can be thinned with water but which is not dissolved by it when dry. It is excellent for painting picture frames

Eraser Use a medium to soft grade to prevent damaging the surface of the mounting card. Keep it clean and pare off any hard skin that develops

Etching A picture made by lines and textures etched into a metal plate by acid. Ink for printing the picture is introduced into the lines, and the surface is wiped clean. A printing press is used to squeeze the etched plate against a piece of damp paper. The shape of the metal plate is clearly seen beyond the boundary of the picture

Filler Proprietary brands of car-body repair filler described as 'elastic' are excellent for repairing moulding. A basic paste and a small quantity of hardener are mixed together; it takes about five minutes to set. It can be cut 'cheese-hard' and sanded to shape when set. Adheres extremely well

Gilder's cushion A card or board padded with a thin layer of cotton wool and covered with soft leather, suede-side up. It is held by a loop at the back

Gilder's knife A broad steel knife with a crisp, angled end. An old, large bread knife or a modified large, palette knife or spatula might serve instead

Gilder's tip A very broad flat brush with the hair set in a flat card handle

Glass Glass about 2–3 mm ($\frac{1}{8}$ in.) thick is suitable for pictures. Non-reflective glass has a finely dimpled surface, which, while not greatly changing the appearance of the picture, limits reflections

Glass cutter A special tool, often with a rotatable head, giving several replacement cutting wheels

Glue Four types are useful to the framer: rubber-based adhesive is suitable to stick paper to paper or material to card; wood-working glue (synthetic) is white when fresh and clear when dry; impact – applied to both surfaces to be joined – when part-dry makes an instant bond when the two surfaces are brought together; rabbit-skin glue – bought by the sheet or granulated – is dissolved in water. Rabbit-skin glue has a short life when wet, quickly going bad. If burnt in heating, it will lose its adhesive quality; use a double boiler to prevent this

Gold leaf Extremely thin sheets of gold are sold in books, containing about 25 leaves. Variations of colour are obtainable, ranging from 16 to $23\frac{1}{2}$ carat. Silver and metal leaf are also available

Gouache Pigment carried in a water-based glue and applied in opaque coats. White pigment is used to make lighter tones. Poster paint is generally similar but may use a coarser pigment

Ground An underlying coating on a painting or frame. It is essential for adhering paint to canvas or gold leaf to wood

Gummed paper White or brown paper with a water-soluble gum on one side. Acid-free gummed paper is available which is not likely to discolour or form spots in ageing and is thus suitable for special conservation work

Hammer A cross-pein 100 gm ($3\frac{1}{2}$ oz) is the most useful in framing. This has a thin, flat head unlike the domed head of the ball-pein. Take care with the cross-pein – its thin, flat head can make nasty dents if misused

Japan gold size A proprietary mixture of copal varnish and dryers. Used for gilding

Knife An all-purpose craft knife with a good large handle to grip. Replaceable blades essential. Some small craft knives used for modelmaking are too fragile for cutting mounts

Lithography Lithography was invented in 1798 by Senefelder and has become one of the most versatile of printing processes. On a stone block or metal plate a design is drawn or painted with a greasy chalk. While the remainder of the surface is kept damp, printing ink adheres to the drawn areas alone, owing to the antipathy of grease and water. It is then possible to take a print of the design.

Masonry bit See **Tungsten bit**

Masonry bolt A bolt which, on being tightened, expands part of its casing to fit tightly into the hole in which it is placed

Masonry nails Nails especially toughened to penetrate brick

Mirror plate A metal T-shaped plate, part of which is screwed to the object and part to the wall

Mitre Joint of two pieces of wood at an angle of 90°, with the line of the junction bisecting this angle

Mitre box A box made of wood or metal which guides a saw for cutting mitres

Mount A surround to a picture – usually made of stiff card

Oil paint Pigment carried in a mixture of oils, used transparently or opaquely. Because the oils change their chemical state by combining with oxygen, they dry from the outside inwards. The final drying time can be many months

Pencils Use a medium grade – 2B. Hard grades damage the surface of cards; very soft grades lose their precise point

Pins *Panel pins/moulding pins* – thin round nails with very small heads

Pliers Metal pincers with flat or pointed jaws and a wire-cutting notch

Poster colour See **Gouache**

Print A broad term concerned with a process in which the artist prepares the picture personally and then makes identical or near identical prints by the chosen process. An edition will usually be of a stated number, and each print numbered. Artists' proofs are works made before the numbered edition. Many commercial processes have been added to the range but these tend to be directed to mass production

Putty There are many proprietary brands of adhesive putty available for temporarily fixing paper to another surface. A quantity the size of a match head is enough to stop a picture slipping under glass

Rabbet The hollow step in the back of a frame section to take the picture

Rulers A straight-edge with a variety of measuring marks. In many cases an actual ruler is not required, but a straight-edged, long piece of wood can be excellent. The measurements marked are not in themselves important as they simply serve as a location for a point

Ruling pen A pen with two adjustable parallel blades which will carry ink or watercolour between them. Ruling pens produce an even line, but considerable practice is needed to avoid blots. A *stilo-tipped draughtsman's pen* has a fine tube for a nib which produces an even line. Available in a variety of widths, this pen is less likely to blot and can be used in conjunction with watercolour

Sandpaper A paper covered with abrasive sand. Obtainable in varying degrees of roughness. S = coarse, M = medium and F = fine. The higher the grit number, the finer the sandpaper will be. Emery paper or cloth covered with corundum is similar but more satisfactory for use on metal

Saw A back saw used in framing (sometimes called a tenon saw) with a 300 mm (12 in.) blade and about 16 teeth per 25 mm (1 in.)

Screw eyes A screw which has a ring at its head

Screws Many types are suitable. When using countersunk screws, those with a cross-shaped slot look better than those with a single slot. Some types have a coarse thread and twist in quickly, which can be an advantage. In hard frames, brass screws and screw eyes can break off unless a pilot hole is made first

Set square A transparent triangle with one 90° angle and two 45° angles

Silk screen A print created by the use of a fine material screen and inks. The areas not required to print are blocked out. On a coarse screen, dots can be seen where the ink has passed through the gaps in the weave

Sizes

International metric sizes (mm)	Imperial approximate equivalent (in.)
A1 841 × 594	33 × 23
A2 594 × 420	23 × 16$\frac{1}{2}$
A3 420 × 297	16$\frac{1}{2}$ × 11$\frac{1}{2}$
A4 297 × 210	11$\frac{1}{2}$ × 8$\frac{1}{4}$

Slip A narrow addition to the inside edge of a frame

Stretcher A wooden frame on which a canvas is tacked. The corners are tongue and grooved and, by use of wedges, are expandable for tightening the canvas. A range of sizes is available, and special lengths can be ordered. The sections of stretchers can vary, so check their compatibility

Tape Masking tape is most useful for general purposes because it has mild but good sticking power – e.g., use for sealing the back of a frame. Clear sticky tape is not good for it can stain and become very brittle.

T-square A wood straight-edge with a cross piece at 90° at one end

Tungsten bit A specially-tipped bit for cutting into hard brick

Vice A metal or wood adjustable clamp, which can be fixed to a table. Wooden facing pieces should be added – most metal vices provide screw fixing holes

Vignette An image which is not a firm rectangle but a shape made of the objects involved. The area tends to occupy an oval

Watercolour paint Pigment carried in water-based glue and applied in transparent or semi-transparent washes, allowing the paper to affect the final tones obtained

Weights   1 gm = 0.035 oz   1 oz = 28.35 gm
            1 kg = 2.2046 lb   1 lb = 0.4536 kg

White spirit Double rectified paraffin, sometimes called turps substitute. Excellent, for it leaves no sticky resinous deposit.

Index